Seven Steps for Handling Grief

Because You Care

Barbara Russell Chesser, PhD

New York Times and *USA Today*
Bestselling Author

SUNSTONE
PRESS

SANTA FE

Sunstone books may be purchased for educational, business, or sales promotional use.
For information please write: Special Markets Department, Sunstone Press,
P.O. Box 2321, Santa Fe, New Mexico 87504-2321.

Book and Cover design › Vicki Ahl
Body typeface › California FB ♦ Display typeface › Coronet
Printed on acid free paper

Library of Congress Cataloging-in-Publication Data

Chesser, Barbara.
  Seven steps for handling grief : because you care / by Barbara Russell Chesser.
     p. cm.
  Includes bibliographical references.
  ISBN 978-0-86534-705-2 (softcover : alk. paper)
  1. Grief. 2. Bereavement--Psychological aspects. I. Title.
  BF575.G7C464 2009
  155.9'37--dc22
                              2009038114

WWW.SUNSTONEPRESS.COM
SUNSTONE PRESS / POST OFFICE BOX 2321 / SANTA FE, NM 87504-2321 /USA
(505) 988-4418 / ORDERS ONLY (800) 243-5644 / FAX (505) 988-1025

Seven Steps
for
Handling Grief

Contents

Foreword

ֆ

*H*urting is human, but unfortunately most of us do not know how to help when a grief-stricken friend is suffering. We feel a sense of helplessness.

Most of us, however, are caring, compassionate human beings who sincerely want to help—if we just knew what to do and how to do it. This book provides practical ideas about what we can do when a friend faces one of life's most shattering experiences—the death of a loved one.

Based on years of research and numerous interviews with people who have experienced painful deathblows, the author tells how people might reach out in ways all of us are capable of to help bereaved friends and relatives. The insightful and heartwarming illustrations in the book come straight from real life.

Much thought and serious study underlie the suggestions and substance of *Seven Steps for Handling Grief*. This book is psychologically valid and spiritually sound. All suggestions given are based on universal human needs.

The suggestions in this book can also aid in sustaining those who are stricken with grief over other losses besides death such as divorce or other broken relationships, termination of a job, decline of financial security, a move from familiar surroundings and friends, the "empty nest" syndrome experienced by some when grown children leave the home, or the destruction of a home and personal belongings caused by a fire or horrendous storm. Other heart-wrenching losses, or "little deaths" as Elisabeth Kübler-Ross calls them, may include having to put an aging parent in a nursing home, having a baby with multiple handicaps, amputation or loss of the use of an arm or leg, loss of sight or hearing, or reduced social standing resulting from moral improprieties or imprisonment of a family member.

Some other situations in which caring individuals can offer solace involve the death of dreams, such as the inability to have a child, unfulfilled commitments, and failing to secure a desired job or promotion. The poet John Greenleaf Whittier captured the poignancy of these unfulfilled dreams:

> For all sad words of tongue or pen,
> The saddest are these: "It might have been!"

Seven Steps for Handling Grief is not sad; rather it is practical and helpful. The book describes sensitive life-enhancing acts of reaching out in friendship to the grief-stricken. Everyone should read this book, for all of us will need its message sooner or later. I believe in the power of positive thinking, and I like this book—*Seven Steps for Handling Grief*—because it is written with compassionate understanding and empathy, offering positive ways that individuals can help the bereaved.

The author is uniquely qualified to write this book. She earned a Doctor of Philosophy degree in human development and behavior, and has an outstanding record in university teaching, research and writing, and counseling. The author has herself personally experienced many of the losses about which she writes and is therefore provided with an unusual personal and professional background. From a storehouse of knowledge and experience, Dr. Chesser offers a definitive and moving book that is well designed to meet an important human need.

Thomas Huxley once said, "The great end of life is not knowledge but action." I believe the real measure of a book is whether it prompts people to take meaningful and appropriate action. *Seven Steps for Handling Grief* will help you do just that—it will help you take steps to turn grief of futility and despair into understanding, faith, and hope.

—Norman Vincent Peale
June, 1987
Pawling, New York

Acknowledgments

❧

The encouragement, insights, and knowledge as well as the tragedies and triumphs of many are woven into the fabric of this book.

To the numerous survivors of grief who shared with me the experiences of life's darkest hours, I owe immeasurable appreciation, for they made this book possible. They, in turn, always expressed heartfelt gratitude for friends who helped turn their darkness into light.

To the late Dr. Norman Vincent Peale, I owe a special debt of gratitude. The words in his foreword, written years before his death, capture his wisdom and are timeless. But my appreciation goes further than the foreword to this book. As a thirteen-year-old, I found my life turned around by Dr. Peale's book, *The Power of Positive Thinking for Young People*. Since then his other books and writings have influenced my life tremendously both in times of joy and sorrow.

To other counselors, clergy, and individuals who shared out of their experiences with grief, I owe boundless thanks. Some are recognized by name within the book; others preferred not to be identified.

To the University of Nebraska I will always be grateful for the support of my research on family crises. That research was the genesis not only of this book but of my awareness of the many human hurts people endure and how friends and family members can take meaningful steps to help heal that hurt, in turn enriching their own lives.

To my mother, grandmother, sisters, and brothers I owe immense gratitude for their magnificent example that life can go on, and that it can go on richly and fully, in spite of painful losses.

To the late Philip B. Osborne, Senior Staff Editor, *Reader's Digest*, I salute his wisdom in recognizing the need for imparting information on practical ways to help those who grieve. I also appreciate his expertise in shaping the information into a well-received article for *Reader's Digest*. Finally, I value Phil's spark of genius in suggesting, "This should be a book!"

To Kelley Smith Higgs I am indebted to her for her extraordinary standard of excellence and positive attitude and assistance.

To my husband, Del, I express my appreciation for his unfailing support and unflappable patience as I edited and re-edited the manuscript he affectionately called my "mission and ministry." He knew that many people need the message in this book.

To other family members and friends who rounded out the circle of love and encouragement that the writing of this book required, I say a fathomless "Thanks." Their prayers and confidence emboldened me when interviewing and writing became difficult and discouraging.

To the compassionate individuals who read this book and use it to help someone else, I commend you for caring enough to do something to help, for that is what this book is all about. May your life in turn be richly blessed.

NOTE: To my readers who like to understand how references from the Bible are identified, I have specified the translation or version with each citation if the translation is other than *The King James* version. If the quote is from *The King James* version, I have given only the reference. Since I have quoted passages from various versions of the Bible, this decision was made with you in mind. I hope you will find my system "reader friendly."

S*tep 1*
⋘

B*e* Th*ere*
If there's anything I can do, let me know.

iding leisurely through the countryside, my twenty-year-old sister and her husband were enjoying a pleasant Labor Day weekend. Then a drunk driver ran a stop sign—in a few seconds of screeching tires, spraying glass, and a senseless snarl of steel the drunk driver snatched the lives and future of a young couple and robbed an infant son of both parents. The drunk driver and his companions staggered away from the accident, unharmed.

Decades later on the anniversary weekend of this agonizing double tragedy, I visited my mother. She was elderly; we did not discuss Janet and Robert's deaths. We reminisced about the happy times. Neither did we discuss my father's death. We spoke only of good memories of him. For me, any discussion of my father has always been of memories others shared, for I was only eight months old when he died in a car wreck November 2, 1941. My father was buried on my mother's

24th birthday, November 6, 1941. A few weeks later, December 7, 1941, Pearl Harbor occurred.

After visiting my mother a few days, I returned home. Then in another few days came September 11, 2001. Four large, commercial American airplanes were hijacked by suicide terrorists. Two of the planes were flown into the World Trade Centers in New York City and one crashed into the Pentagon, in Washington, D.C., while the fourth plane exploded in a Pennsylvania field. Before the tragic day was over, approximately 3,000 people perished—husbands, wives, sons, daughters, other loved ones and friends from eighty nations. In less than two hours, the death toll was more than twice the number killed in Pearl Harbor during this other day of infamy.

A few short weeks later, another tragedy occurred—only minutes after taking off from New York City a plane crashed, snuffing out the lives of several hundred more people. This catastrophe pierced the heart of a nation still numb from September 11—and broke the hearts of many other loving, caring family members and friends of the fatalities.

Even though I have a PhD in human development and behavior, have studied in numerous courses on grief recovery, have taught courses in how to cope with grief, and continue to read countless books on the topic, the emotional aftershocks of these dreadful tragedies riveted my heart and soul just as they did of other people all over the world. The only other time I suffered such searing pain was after my sister and her husband were killed.

Searching for ways to help others—and myself—after the terrible tragedy of losing my sister and her husband, I began an ongoing research project at the university where I taught at the time. Approximately 350 survivors of grief shared their stories and what helped them overcome their grief, and fifty-five grief counselors summarized helpful ways to heal the hurt. From my research—

and that of many other grief experts—I thought that my mother captured the essence of their accumulated wisdom when she replied to someone's question on the fiftieth year anniversary of my father's death. This person asked how long it takes to get over the death of a loved one. My mother responded simply, "You don't ever get over it. You just learn to live with it."

Based on the experience of numerous losses, my mother went on to extol the power of some practical gestures of caring people. Her explanation and the wise counsel of all the experts emphasize that recovery of inconsolable grief depends on a variety of healing influences. There is no silver bullet to eradicate terrorism, no single action to prevent incompetent drivers from killing people like my father, and no one law that will keep drunk drivers from causing senseless deaths like those of my sister and her husband. Similarly, there is no one dramatic gesture or pearl of wisdom that can be uttered to heal the heartache of loss.

There are, however, many thoughtful acts that loved ones, friends, co-workers, and others can take that will convey care and concern and over time ease the pain inflicted by the death blow and other heartbreaking losses.

Being There Is a Good Beginning

After my sister and her husband were killed, well wishers poured into our house, offering consolation for the inexpressible grief and outrage we all felt. Many kind, caring people said, "If there's anything I can do, let me know." These age-old words are nearly always offered whenever a friend, relative, or colleague suffers a death in the family or some other catastrophe. Most well-meaning people are at a loss to know what else to say or do. The numerous people I interviewed emphasized that grief-stricken people often don't even know what they must do, much less what someone else might do for them, or how they can be comforted and consoled. Being there is one important step caring people can take.

Being there is a good beginning, for taking time out of your own busy schedule to go to the hospital or to the home of someone who has just died or suffered some other inconsolable loss shows that you care about the survivors and that you are concerned about their feelings. Your taking this first step and being there shows that you are willing to share the painful emotions of grief—shock, bewilderment, anguish, desolation. In addition, your being there indicates to the survivors that you value the life of the deceased. Your willingness to be vulnerable demonstrates that you care about the survivors and are willing to cry with them.

Being there can also soften the hurt of an anticipated death. This is "the time when the relatives walk up and down the hospital hallways, tormented by the waiting. This is the time when it is too late for words, and yet the time when the relatives cry for help—with or without words."[1] A few years ago, for example, Carol Adams saw her husband, Joel, struck down in the prime of life by a fast-spreading cancer.

At the time, he was a lieutenant colonel stationed at a large air force base on the East Coast. A short time before Joel died, one of his friends, a fellow officer, came to the hospital with Carol. After a brief visit with Joel, the friend and soon-to-be widow walked from the room and down the hall. "This is a terrible time for both of us," Joel's friend said, tears in his eyes. Then the two hugged, clasped hands, and finally cried together. "By his taking time to be with me and to share his tears with me," Carol says, "he told me how much and how deeply he cared. It helps to know that the death of someone you love is also a significant loss for others."

Being with a close friend or relative at the moment of death can also be comforting. Most people in America die in hospitals, so we are often robbed of the opportunity to be with them when they die. In some cases, perhaps, this may be better, but one expert made this observation about people who were ushered out at the last: "They felt cheated, wondering whether there might not have been a last contact, a word, a glance."[2] People who have been with loved ones at the time of death often describe a feeling of peace about it. As one man put it, "I was glad that I was at my dad's bedside when he died. I'd like to think he knew I was there with him. I was pretty shaken, but a friend was there with me."

Your being there—before a death, at the time of death, or at any time afterward—is a tangible reminder to the bereaved that he or she is not alone. One of the painful emotions surrounding a death is a feeling of abandonment, of being "cut off" from the dead loved one. The September 11 catastrophe not only robbed countless people of their lives; it robbed them of their deaths—not to be able to say good-bye to loved ones, not to be able to view the body, not to have any tangible evidence that the loved one truly is dead. Grief will be compounded in these cases, and the tender outreaching of friends and relatives is even more important. The presence of friends can show the grief-stricken that there are still people who love them, people to whom they can relate—that there are still meaningful relationships.

Later in the grief process, especially after the shock has worn off, your being there is concrete evidence that life goes on—this is what the experts call "continuity." All this "being there" constitutes "emotional support." Or we could simply call it love, and love expressed in this way by caring friends truly does help soften the deathblow. Also by being there, you will be able to see a myriad of other things that need to be done—many created by the death itself.

Practical Ways to Offer Comfort

Helping the bereaved at first may involve something as simple as being at their house to answer the phone or making calls to notify others of the death. Or you might accompany someone who must tell an aging or ill person about the death.

Helping organize the handling of food brought in from neighbors and friends is always a practical way anyone can help. Keeping a record of who brings the food will simplify writing thank-you notes later. Labeling the dishes or containers for easy return to owners or actually returning the dishes as they become empty is also helpful. If there is an overabundance of food, freezing some of it in disposable or microwave containers with labels and directions for preparation will provide convenience later on. Furnishing disposable plates and drink containers will aid kitchen cleanup. Other practical ways of offering solace will come to mind if you are around the bereaved.

Appendix A lists "Actions to Take Before Death and Afterward." Some of these must be done immediately, and some obviously can wait a while. What you offer to do will depend, of course, upon your relationship to the deceased and to the grievers as well as upon your abilities and interests. The Golden Rule serves well in this situation: simply consider what would be comforting to you if you were the bereaved person. For instance, while one newly-widowed friend of mine was away from her house making funeral arrangements, several friends straightened her home. They washed and dried the towels and hung them back fresh and clean, vacuumed throughout the house, made the beds, mowed the lawn, and put a pot of colorful chrysanthemums near the front door. The widow was visibly touched—she and her husband had always taken pride in their home and lawn. As she looked over what her friends had done in just an hour or so, her tears of gratitude turned to a gentle chuckle. "Doug would have loved this," she said.

Another woman I heard about arrived at a home where a death had recently occurred and, with a few quiet words and a squeeze of her hand, passed along a note. It indicated the hours she was available for picking up friends or relatives at the airport and also offered the use of her spare bedroom and a convertible couch in her den.

Encouraging the bereaved to rest periodically is another practical way to help them. At the time of a death those who have been close by may already be physically and emotionally exhausted. When my grandfather died, for example, he had been in the hospital five weeks. My grandmother had spent endless hours day and night by his bedside. After his death many relatives and friends came by to see my grandmother. She wanted to see them all, of course, but after two days of visiting with a steady stream of people, she was exceedingly weary. A kind friend ushered Grandmother to her bedroom. Then she helped her put on her robe and lay down beside her for a refreshing rest from the well-wishers. Thoughtful friends and relatives understood that grieving people need some rest and respite and did not take offense. But sometimes a helpful friend must take the initiative.

Well-meaning friends may take initiatives that are more harmful than helpful—for instance, encouraging the grief-stricken to take tranquilizers or other mood-altering drugs to blot out the anguish. Evidence clearly indicates that heavy sedation tends to postpone feelings, not remove them. Unfortunately, these delayed feelings often surface later in less appropriate settings when other people may not be as understanding and compassionate, for they think the mourner has already worked through most of the grief.[3] One physician said simply, "Drugs may not be able to fill the void, and in the final analysis they may not be anywhere near as effective as the calming capacity of human friendship."[4]

A Time to Grieve

So, one of the most helpful things a friend can do for the grief-stricken is to allow the genuine expression of grief. The writer of Ecclesiastes made this wise observation hundreds of years ago, and it is as sound today as it was then: "There is a right time for everything: A time to be born, a time to die, . . . A time to cry, . . . A time to grieve. . . ." (Ecclesiastes 3:1, 2, 4, *The Living Bible*).

Contrary to the spirit of these verses, we Americans take great pride in "holding together" and "keeping a stiff upper lip." Some of us remember that long-ago bleak November 22, 1963, when John Fitzgerald Kennedy—"JFK" to many of us—was shot down by an assassin. We all marveled at how well Jackie "held up" during the awful days that followed. The clips showing Jackie during those days were shown again when John Kennedy, Jr., his wife, Carolyn, and Carolyn's sister died in a tragic plane crash.

Because the whole nation—indeed the entire world—had their eyes focused on Jackie, perhaps there was value in her being the stoic model at that time in history. But in most cases denial of our sadness and other grief-related emotions is unhealthy and does not help heal the hurt at all. The unashamed sharing of grief and tears over the horrendous destruction of buildings and lives September 11 has, in contrast, helped the healing and bonded our nation in unity—that in itself is a healing force.

In *Peace of Mind* Joshua Liebman accepts the ecclesiastic wisdom and devotes a chapter to "Grief's Slow Wisdom," emphasizing the importance of expressing grief. He summarizes, "It is not those outbursts which harm but the complete avoidance of them, which scars and tears the fabric of the inner soul."[5] Many of the grievers in my research study verified this; they spoke of long ago griefs that healed only after coming to grips with them. I was beginning to realize the wisdom of that by acknowledging my father's death, asking questions about him, and allowing myself to feel the pain of having lost a father years before I was old enough to comprehend this sad loss. A young widow's experience validates the importance of expressing grief:

> If I had been able to burst into wild tears, it would have done us all a lot of good. The children probably would have cried, too, and we would all have been sobbing away. I would have been able to cry and to say, "We hate it a lot. It's a bum rap." But all my energies, then and later, were exerted in holding myself together. I always had this Humpty Dumpty fantasy that if I were ever to allow myself to crack, no one, not "all the King's men" could ever put me back together again. I'm beginning to learn how wrong I was. Emotions can strengthen you, not splinter you. To express emotions is healthier than to repress them.[6]

Shakespeare expressed the same notion in his play, *King Henry VI*, when one of the characters said simply, "To weep is to make less the depth of grief."

Different Ways of Expressing Grief

Grief may be expressed in a multiplicity of feelings depending on the personality of the grief-stricken, how the grief-stricken think they "ought to" react, the circumstances surrounding the death, and a variety of other influences. These feelings nearly always, however, include "the shocking blow of the loss in itself, the numbing effects of the shock, the struggle between fantasy and reality," and then "the breakthrough of the flood of grief."[7]

These feelings will come at different times for different people, but perceptive friends who allow their expression are invaluable at any time. Since my own father, for instance, died when I was an infant, my grieving and yearning to talk about him came years later. But the longing was nevertheless intense. Mourning my father's death took a special turn, perhaps because he had died long before I could comprehend what death was all about. What I craved to speak about was not his death but his life—how he and my mother met, why he enjoyed ranching, what he said on various occasions, what he laughed about, how he was affable (he liked people and they liked him), and how he enjoyed life until his untimely death. Recalling the life of the dead is an important part of resolving grief. Besides, we all need these memories to hold onto. Lisa Beamer, the young widow whose husband heroically helped prevent a fourth plane from flying into a building on September 11 (and killing untold others) said that people who knew Todd will share memories of him with her children as they grow older, and "that will help keep his legacy alive."

The former Chief of the Department of Psychiatry of the Harvard University Medical School, Dr. Erich Lindemann pointed out a paradox that may explain my behavior and that of many others who want and need to talk about a deceased loved one. "The only way to survive a crisis . . . to work through a loss," he emphasized, "is to be keenly and openly aware of it." He continued, "The only way of forgetting is through remembering."[8] The American poet Robert Frost put it this way: "The best way out is always through."

It's Okay to Cry

Realizing that the best way is to deal directly and openly with grief, you can help a friend by encouraging him or her to express grief and all its accompanying feelings. The most common response to grief is crying. The experts contend that crying releases emotional tension and is essential to "the breakthrough of the flood of grief." The sharing of grief and tears during the aftermath of September 11 truly demonstrated that tears are not only "okay," they bond us together as caring, feeling human beings. An insightful book called *The Courage to Grieve* points out that "Tears are then the jewels of remembrance, sad but glistening with the beauty of the past. So grief in its bitterness marks the end, but it also is praise to the one who is gone."[9] Also, remember that Jesus' response to Lazarus' death was crying. The account in the Bible says simply, "Jesus wept." (John 11:35) Why shouldn't we allow the same healthful expression from our friends or family—or complete strangers?

Knowing how to help the grief-stricken express their grief—how to help them to cry—is not always easy. One of my professors in graduate school told me and others in a class on family crisis how her husband had died when she was about six months pregnant. Many well-intentioned people, as well as her parents, offered advice similar to this: "You must be brave for the baby's sake" and "You have to carry on for your baby." They thought these words would encourage her to have something to look forward to rather than dwelling on her anguish at her husband's death.

This dear woman, who was in her early sixties when she shared this personal story with us, said she walked around like an "emotional zombie," as she put it, until one weekend a close friend took her to visit her husband's grave for the first time since his burial. She read the inscription on the tombstone, and the reality of the death of her husband—the father of her two-month-old daughter—hit her like a falling wall. "All my pent-up feelings," she said, "began crumbling." She related how she cried almost incessantly for hours into the night. She then cried spasmodically for over a week and then less and less often. Crying, she said, lifted a heavy burden from her and was truly a breakthrough in her grief recovery.

Some parents who have had a stillborn baby provide other examples of how crying helps handle the grief and heal the hurt. Their stories, shared in a moving book, *Stillborn: The Invisible Death*, describe the long, difficult journey of families mourning a stillbirth. Outsiders frequently maintain a wall of silence, according to these parents, as though there had never been a life—or a death. John DeFrain and the other co-authors (who all suffered stillbirths) tell how this denial reaction from friends and relatives prolongs the grief. Here is what one distraught mother said:

> After leaving the hospital (ten days), I tried to fulfill people's expectations of me. So, I put my emotions on "automatic control" and performed the usual everyday things of life for about three months. My doctor's concerned attention caused him to ask help from my mother. He felt that I must have some relief from my pent-up grief. . . . She came one day to my door unannounced. . . . I wept unrestrainedly for hours. . . . I'm sure this was a great help to me, but three months is a long time, and the early tears I should have been allowed are still behind my eyelids, and the lonely hurt is still a hard lump somewhere in the center of me.[10]

Men may especially need assurance from a friend or relative that it is okay to cry. One young father shares how consoling it was to have that freedom:

> Other than my wife, I would have to say that it was my father who helped me the most. He, like many other dads, brought his sons up to be strong and not to

cry, which I had never seen him do but once before. He and my mom were at the hospital the night our baby died. He was the first person I saw. . . . I threw my arms around him as I used to as a child when I was scared, and we cried. . . . And I knew that he was there, just as always. It was a great help to me.[11]

Another father whose child had died was asked what was most helpful to him. He replied simply, "My father was helpful because he cried with me."[12]

These men were fortunate to have fathers who were strong enough to cry with them. Some men who suffer a significant loss are not so lucky. Men are all too frequently victims of what have been called "The Commandments of Masculinity." In small, subtle (and sometimes not-so-subtle) ways, we pressure men to keep on their "real man" macho masks. At the time of a death, we may be particularly guilty of expecting men to be "brave"—which in our society means showing no emotion. Lamentable also is our serious mistake of equating crying with "breaking down." What we are really doing is depriving men of their own humanity, of their right to own up to their emotions, of their right to express these feelings, of their right to receive comfort and solace from friends and relatives. We more generally allow all these rights to women but not to men. This is a case of a double standard in which men are cruelly victimized. Here are the hurtful, unfair "Commandments of Masculinity" that are imposed upon a man:

He shall not cry.
He shall not display weakness.
He shall not need affection or gentleness or warmth.
He shall comfort but not desire comforting.
He shall be needed but not need.

He shall touch but not be touched.
He shall be steel not flesh.
He shall be inviolate in his manhood.
He shall stand alone.[13]

One man, who is well into retirement—we'll call him John—has suffered interminably from "The Commandments of Masculinity." John's wife died when they both were in their early thirties. They had three children, and John, like my professor, felt that he had to be brave for his children's sake. Evidently he had no or few friends or relatives who encouraged him to work out his grief. Moreover perhaps for the reasons suggested by "The Commandments of Masculinity," he denied expression of his innermost hurt, and his grief found detours into other more disruptive problems. In his case, unexpressed grief literally became a disease. Ever since his wife's death, various ailments have befallen him—he has spent endless hours with physicians and an incredible amount of money on medicine. Unfortunately, says Dr. S. I. McMillen, "peace does not come in capsules."[14] This medical doctor says that in many cases illness, including chronic headaches, high blood pressure, heart trouble, and other diseases too numerous to mention, can be traced to unwisely managed grief as a significant contributing cause.

A former state senator who participated in my research project on grief reports no physical ailments caused by his mother's death when he was fourteen. But he does recall feeling very despondent for a long time after his mother's death. He remembers already being filled with typical teenage uncertainties and struggles, and that no one seemed to want to share his grief. "They all assumed," he observes, "that I was a young man and resilient and that I would get over it." He concludes, "I was able to act the part of being brave, but on the inside I was crushed. I desperately needed someone to recognize that I was devastated. I really loved Mother, and her dying was almost more than I could bear. I needed someone to help me handle the awful hurt."

The need to express and share grief extends even to young children, says Catherine Laughlin, a friend and professional colleague I met when we both taught at the University of Nevada in Reno. "Our kids were young when Joe became ill and eventually died," she recalls. "Martin was six and Louise was a couple of years younger. I tried to be brave for their sakes; I said little to them about their father and returned to a normal routine as quickly as I could after their father's death."

Then one evening about six months later, Catherine was reading some bedtime stories to her son and daughter when little Louise suddenly blurted: "Won't Daddy be surprised when he sees how we've grown!" Martin wrinkled his young brow. "Daddy is dead," he said, glaring at his younger sister. "He won't ever come back." Then he added emphatically, "Let's not talk about it ever again!"

That's when Catherine realized that her children had been wrestling with the same emotions that she had been stifling. Right then, she decided they all had to talk. "When we began sharing our feelings openly and experiencing and expressing the full depth of our anguish," she says, "then we finally began to accept the unacceptable." Catherine's experience reinforces the approach Eda LeShan, author and educator, suggests for helping children deal with death: "A child can live through anything so long as he or she is told the truth and is allowed to share with loved ones the natural feelings people have when they are suffering."[15]

Times for Special Sensitivity

As these true stories show, people of all ages and both genders need sincere friends who will help them through their mourning, but—depending on the circumstances of the death—some people may need warm, caring friendship more than others. Death that comes in the fullness of time is, to be sure, a sadness and a loss, but death that comes to a young person, or accidentally or violently, is an even greater shock. A suicide, for example, brings extra excruciating pain.

Every year between fifty thousand and half a million teenagers attempt suicide while five thousand succeed. This is an average of one suicide roughly every two hours! Statistics for older people are equally startling.[16] These statistics represent families who need comforting with even greater perception, sensitivity, concern, and caring.

Consider the story of Mike and Betty and their sixteen-year-old son. They were a typical family; from all outside appearances everything was okay. Mike and Betty thought everything was fine, too. Of course, there were some of the usual ups and downs—some of the tensions that all parents and children experience, some of the disappointments with grades, frustrations with boy-girl relationships, and letdowns in the sports arena. But when Brett left a suicide note in his bedroom, telling his parents he loved them and not to blame themselves, and then drove his white Camaro off a steep cliff to a certain death, his parents were shocked in disbelief. "We felt like horrible parents," Mike says years later. "Over and over we grilled ourselves, searching for what we'd done wrong or what we could've done to have prevented Brett from feeling like suicide was his only escape."

Friends and relatives are generally also stunned at a suicide and do not know what to say or do. To be there is especially helpful. No words, no explanations, no rhetoric are needed, nor do they help. Mike points out, "Friends just being with us helped us know that they still loved us, that we weren't some terrible people who'd done something heinous to deserve this fate." Betty adds, "Parents of Brett's friends who came to be with us were especially helpful. Some people who we thought were friends shunned us—we never saw them or heard from them during the first inconsolable months."

"As time went on," says Mike, "and the shock wore off and the heartsickening reality set in, especially courageous friends stuck it out with us, letting us lean on them and cry out our frustration, our helplessness, and our heartbreak at the starkness of our son's dreadful death."

Thoughtful gestures and caring concern help with the immediate pain when a loved one dies, but it is after most of the friends and relatives have gone home that the numbing shock wears off and the reality of the death and its pangs of grief stab deepest. Friends who are willing to spend a little time and effort can help calm the inner chaos in the long months following a death. In many instances, friends who will draw close when the road gets long and rough are indispensable. My good friend, Bev, for example, recalls how she and her husband, Ken, along with another couple, had enjoyed the day boating on a scenic California lake. The two men had just let their wives out at the dock near their cabin. The women were going to prepare lunch while their husbands took another short spin. About one hundred yards from the shore, Ken's new boat exploded, splintering into literally thousands of pieces. Both men were thrown from the boat. Though shaken, Bob was able to swim to the shore. Ken never came to the surface of the water, and his body was not found for months.

"That was the most miserable time you can imagine—it was a nightmare," Bev says now, decades later. All the decisions that had to be made, especially those involving the legal proceedings against the boat manufacturer, were simply overwhelming, according to Bev. "Tom, a friend of ours who was an attorney, helped tremendously," she says. "He didn't handle the case—an older lawyer who specialized in accidents like this did—but Tom helped me get through it all by assuring me that the lawyer was doing the right thing."

Bev goes on, "I was thankful to have some help—my mind wouldn't work. I couldn't concentrate on all the legal and financial matters. All I could think about was finding Ken's body. Every time the phone rang, I froze. As much as I wanted to know something— the not knowing was awful—I was so afraid of finally hearing the inevitable words, 'Ken is dead. We have found his body.'" She adds, "I sometimes couldn't even manage taking care of my six-month-old baby. Friends would come over and take care of her. They'd cook, they'd straighten things up, they'd let me cry, and we'd cry together. I would have absolutely lost my mind if those wonderful friends hadn't stood by me."

Friends who will listen gently to countless "If onlies" are also a special blessing to many who have lost loved ones. In his book, *Don't Take My Grief Away*, Doug Manning says that it is a natural reaction to search for someone or something to blame when someone dies. "You might fix the blame on the doctor or the hospital—or even on the person who died. Somehow the blame has to be transferred somewhere."[17] He goes on to say that most people transfer the blame to themselves. When this happens, those around the grief-stricken will begin to hear "If only I had . . . " statements:

If only I had been there.
If only I had forced him to go to the doctor.
If only I had been a better husband.
If only I had been a better wife.
If only I had been a better father.
If only I had been a better mother.[18]

These "If onlies" are especially intense—that is, the person endures insufferable guilt—if he or she feels solely responsible for causing the death or solely responsible for not preventing it.

One father, for instance, describes how he felt he had failed his only daughter by not teaching her to swim. She was nine years old when she drowned on a family outing. On top of the unbearable guilt the father already felt for not having taught Jamie to swim was the fact that he had tried but failed to rescue her. She flailed her arms frantically, calling "Daddy, Daddy!" before she went down the final time. A pastor who told me about this calamity said that several very patient friends stayed with the distraught father as he again and again repeated every detail of that horrible episode. They reminded him over and over that he wasn't the only father who had not made sure his nine-year-old daughter could swim. Most of all they simply listened and assured him that he had done all he humanly could.

The wife said that these faithful friends helped her cope, too— for she admits now that she also blamed her husband at first for not being able to get to their daughter in time to save her. "Many grew tired and discouraged, and quit visiting this heartbroken couple," relates the pastor, "but those who kept coming back and kept firmly reminding them that they'd done their best and that was all God, Jamie, or anyone expected—they were friends in the truest sense." They were friends like the one the writer of Proverbs described: "A friend who sticks closer than a brother." (Proverbs 18:24, *Revised Standard Version*)

Sharing Kindred Emotions

A friend who has experienced a similar loss can be especially effective. Thomas Jefferson expressed this idea in a letter to a friend: "Who then can so softly bind up the wound of another as he who has felt the same wound himself?" Most of us, of course, feel inadequate to help in the face of death, and many of us, fortunately, have not had much experience with death. We could say what Betsy Burnham said before her own death: "Only a few times had death's lightning struck close enough to startle me with its thunder."[19]

A person whose family member committed suicide in the past, for instance, would probably more ably help comfort someone grieving over a recent suicide. Only someone who has suffered a suicide in the family can truly say, "I know how you feel." My grandmother used to admonish me with some advice she said was "an old Indian saying." You probably have heard it: "Don't judge someone till you've walked a mile in his moccasins." I think we can stretch our imaginations and apply this to helping someone who has lost a loved one to death. For example, until you have suffered a suicide in your family, or had a loved one killed by a drunk driver, or stood by watching helplessly as someone you love slowly and painfully loses her health and then her life to the ravages of cancer, you simply cannot understand the depths of the emotions caused by these deaths. Similarly, until you have lost a mother or father, or a child, or a mate, you cannot fully comprehend the feelings accompanying that specific loss.

People who have suffered a similar loss can provide the empathy—the genuine sharing of kindred emotions—that may be especially consoling. This observation, for example, was made about parents whose babies were stillborn: "Other parents who have lost babies are quick to come to the support of the stillbirth parents. By writing letters, calling on the phone or any other of a million kindnesses, these good people break the isolation and the terrible loneliness that stillbirth parents can feel. They [persons reaching out] say, in effect, 'We are with you. . . . We really do know.'"[20]

When asked what helped heal the hurt the most, others gave these responses:

> "The best help was talking to a lady who had experienced the same thing."[21]

"Knowing that it happens to many made me feel less alone and less guilty."[22]

"What I appreciated was a chance to talk or cry and not have someone try to lessen my feelings but just accept them at that point."[23]

"A friend whose daughter had died came to visit me . . . it was very comforting. My thought was that she made it and so could I."[24]

"People [who] did not pass the death off as 'fate,' or 'God's will,' or 'for the best.' For the most part, people who have been close to a similar experience made the best listeners and talkers."[25]

Support Organizations

Numerous self-help organizations are based on this notion that those who have experienced a particular loss can help others cope with this same loss. Compassionate Friends, for instance, has chapters all over the United States to help parents cope with the death of a child. Parents who have experienced the death of a child meet together to share, to cry, to encourage, to tell what helped them. Those who are further along in the very difficult journey of grief recovery provide the leadership, usually along with one or more professional grief counselors.

Other self-help or support organizations include ones specifically for widows, for widows of ministers, for parents who have lost a baby to SIDS (Sudden Infant Death Syndrome, or "crib death"), and others. Appendix B provides a list of self-help organizations along with contact information. If you want to help a friend who fits any of these categories, you might look at the organization's Web site or write to or call the organization and see what services it provides. A chapter may be located in your friend's hometown or nearby. Offering to visit the local chapter with your friend and be with him or her may be a turning point in helping heal the hurt.

These organizations fill a significant need and fill it well, as can be seen by the increasing number of them springing up across the United States and in other countries as well. But they can only partially fill the need. Friends and relatives—even those who haven't experienced a similar loss but who care and are concerned—can offer crucial support to the bereaved.

Excuses We All Make

Many people minimize the value of what they could possibly do to aid a grief-stricken person. They are a lot like the cartoon character Charlie Brown when he said, "Life is just too much for me. I've been confused right from the day I was born. I think the whole trouble is that we're thrown into life too fast . . . we're not really prepared." Few of us ever feel adequately prepared to help with grief, and we often make excuses. I know this to be true because I find it very easy to make excuses. Whenever I hear about a death in the family of a colleague or friend, my mind starts turning out well-worn reasons why I should not go to be with that bereaved friend:

> "They wouldn't want to see me."
> "I'm afraid I wouldn't know what to say or do."
> "I'm sure I'd say or do the wrong thing."
> "What would I do if they cry or lose control? I don't want to embarrass them."
> "I might lose control and cry. I don't want to embarrass myself."

The list of excuses to prevent our reaching out goes on endlessly, like a shout in a deep canyon echoing on and on. An underlying psychological barrier to our getting involved with a grief-stricken friend may be our inability to face our own mortality. Visiting with or helping someone whose loved one has died may be a painful reminder that we too shall someday die, and so will those we love.

The psalmist put it succinctly when he said: "What man can live and not see death?" (Psalm 89:43, *New American Standard Bible*) When we are able to see death as a "friendly companion on life's journey—gently reminding [us] not to wait till tomorrow to do what [we] mean to do,"[26] then we will be able to comfort those who grieve.

A sad example of denial of death and unresolved grief was a woman in her sixties who had never been to a funeral since her father died when she was eight years old. Her mother at the time was shattered and did not know how to grieve or how to help her daughter express her grief. Others who might have helped the youngster merely admonished her by their words and attitude to "Be brave for your mother's sake." This woman's denial of death and any emotions related to it began early in her life, and she grew up emotionally immobilized, going about "business as usual" when anyone died—and sometimes even working harder. Her way of coping with a death was to look everywhere but at death and at all the emotions that death evokes.

Her looking in the wrong places, so to speak, reminds me of a Sufi story about the mullah who was out in the street on his hands and knees, searching the ground. A friend came by and asked, "Mullah, what are you doing in the street on your hands and knees?" He answered, "I'm hunting for my house key." The friend offered, "I'll help you. Where did you last have your key?" His answer: "Over there by the door." Perplexed, the friend then asked, "Why are you searching here if you last saw your key over there by the door?" Mullah responded, "Because it is too dark over there by the door . . . there is more light here."

Stages of Grief

Realizing that bereaved people go through stages of grief may also help us to comfort them. Some experts describe ten stages of grief recovery, while others express them in three steps. One of the first persons to describe these stages was Elisabeth Kübler-Ross, well known for her study of the stages that dying people go through. She contends that all bereaved persons go through similar stages: denial and isolation, anger, bargaining, depression, and acceptance.[27] Collin M. Parkes in his *Bereavement: Studies of Grief in Adult Life* outlines the stages in this way: denial, separation anxiety, anger and guilt, depression, and acceptance.[28] The author of *The Courage to Grieve* summarizes these stages by saying, "We learn to face the reality and pain of our loss, to say good-bye, to restore ourselves, and to reinvest in life once again."[29] The following overview of the stages of grief recovery may help you handle your own grief and help others handle theirs:

First Stage: Shock

When a loss occurs, even though the grief-stricken may have expected it, they are initially shocked. This shock marks the first stage of grief. The grief-stricken may emotionally deny that there has been a loss, or they may try to rationalize the effects of the loss by saying that this is probably the best outcome possible. As the loss is gradually acknowledged in a realistic way, the grief-stricken will move on to the second stage of grief.

Second Stage: Protest

During the second stage of grief, after the shock has worn off, the bereaved may feel helpless and out of control. They may feel overwhelmed with self-pity, anger, anxiety, and guilt. They may feel angry with themselves or with God—or both. They may ask over and over, "Why did it have to happen?" or "What have I done to deserve this?" Frequent mood swings are common during this period. The bereaved may want to isolate themselves from others, or they may be terrified if left alone.

Third Stage: Despair

This stage is extremely difficult. The bereaved feel the deep pain of depression and sadness related to the loss. All of a sudden they feel terribly alone, terribly confused, terribly depressed and helpless with so many burdens. Life seems to have lost its meaning. They may feel they are losing their minds. Constantly they think of the deceased person or the loss in their life. They may cry at nothing or laugh at anything. They may develop physical pains and even medical problems. They may experience a general feeling of weakness. They may have feelings of suffocation and self-pity. There are the threads of separation—the work of saying good-bye— so that the value and importance of the deceased can become a rational, comfortable part of the bereaved's future life.

Fourth Stage: Resolution

The last stage of grief is the step toward recovery and resolution. The bereaved reach this point when they can think of the loss without feelings that overwhelm them and tear them apart; they lose their constant sorrow, they have bittersweet memories, but they do not completely engulf them. They regain a sense of mastery in their life. They again find new meaning in love for others, their job, their family, and friends. They are again in charge most of the time, and the future looks brighter. In short, there has been an emotional acceptance of the loss.

Knowing and understanding some of these typical reactions to death may help you be more sensitive to your friends' feelings or to your own. It may help you to respond in ways that will meet their needs or yours and help heal the hurt during each of these stages. Knowing that each person goes through the stages in his or her own timetable will also be helpful. In addition, remember that the grief-stricken may regress to former stages or even react in ways characteristic of several stages at one time. Throughout all the stages allow your friends to follow Doug Manning's advice in *Don't Take My Grief Away*:

> The best thing I can say is to feel what you feel. The danger is that you will decide you should not have such feelings and that you are, therefore, either bad or crazy.
>
> The truth is that these feelings will be there. To bury them does not cause them to go away. To deny them does not mean they are not there. The feelings will be there—so let them be there.[30]

Sylvia had suffered a painful loss. She knew very well how helpful it was to have friends who let feelings "be there." Then a friend suffered a similar loss. Here is what Sylvia told her grief-stricken friend:

You don't have to be strong or logical or sensible, or any of the things you think you have to be. For me, it turned out to be better when I didn't try to fight the pain but let it roll over me like a giant tidal wave and carry me along with it, until it spent its fury and dropped me gasping but alive on the shores of sanity. And, like any storm, it gradually died. The waves crashed farther and farther apart, and somewhere, without my being aware of it, life became worth living again.[31]

Personality Upheaval

Before life becomes worth living again, most bereaved persons go through some dreadfully rough times. New personality traits may surprise friends and relatives. They may even startle the bereaved. Grief-stricken persons may be vulnerable, defensive, sensitive, and unreasonable. At the same time they need reassurance, affirmation, protection, time to recoup, and help in mustering up courage to plan for the future. Numerous individuals I interviewed admitted they thought at times throughout their grief they might be losing their minds. This feeling is common enough that one author entitled a chapter in a book on death and grief "Is It Ever 'Normal' to Be 'Crazy'?"[32]

Some even think about suicide. Grieving people may need to be reminded that these are just thoughts, and that they are not necessarily going to act on them. Unfortunately, the suicide rate is higher among people who have suffered some traumatic loss—all the more reason we should understand this reaction to grief. One person who was seventeen when her idolized twenty-year-old brother was killed later offered some valuable insights:

The wish to die is partly a wish for reunion with the dead loved one. Thoughts of dying are also an imaginary way to gain relief from the pain of grief. Suicidal thoughts may be the result of unexpressed guilt or anger, and they serve as self-punishing ideas. Since life does not seem very meaningful at the time of mourning, it is natural to consider death as an alternative. Considering suicide is also one way to come to terms with the fact of loss and death. The thinking is something like this: If I can consider and tolerate the idea of my own death, perhaps death itself will not seem so frightening or so hard for me to endure. Maybe then I'll accept this loss.[33]

Grief Lasts a Long Time

Working through the painful, tumultuous stages of grief and finally accepting the loss takes longer than most people expect. Bereaved individuals need extended doses of patient understanding, warm friendship, and acceptance of their "wild and crazy thoughts as well as their bouts with despair and depression," as one recovering mourner put it.

Some individuals are, of course, able to adjust more quickly than others, but just when we think our mourning friend is doing great—then comes a setback. Here is how one person put it:

Human pain does not let go of its grip at one point in time. Rather, it works its way out of our consciousness over time. There is a season of sadness. A season of anger. A season of tranquility. A season of hope. But seasons do not follow one another in lockstep. The winters and springs of one's life are all jumbled together in a puzzling array. One day we feel as though the dark clouds have lifted, but the next day they have returned. One moment we can smile, but a few hours later the tears emerge. It is true that as we take two steps forward in our journey, we may take one or more steps backward. But when one affirms that the spring thaw will arrive, the winter winds seem to lose some of their punch.[34]

One of my university colleagues told me about one of her students whose fiancé was killed in Iraq; the student said her friends helped her survive the "winter winds" of grief as she rode an emotional roller coaster the first year after her loss:

> I'd pull myself together, thinking, "I'm going to make it." Then the cement that had been holding me together would crumble. My friends never knew what to expect—neither did I. I must've been awful to be around. Thank goodness some of my friends understood that when I was the most irascible and intolerable was when I needed their consolation, love, and friendship the most.

The bereaved need warm, supportive friendship that first year after a death, for some of the sharpest piercing pain comes after the initial shock and numbness wear off. My family's experience bears this out. My mother recalled that when the people were gone, after Janet and Robert's funeral, "An awful emptiness filled the house." Most of her friends, she said, seemed to get back quickly into their own routines. But several people kept returning. "Those short and often unannounced visits," she said, "took some of the sting out of the intolerably lonely days and nights." For example, Joanna, one of Janet's friends, would pop in on her way to the grocery store or on other errands. Once she came by to bring some snapshots of Janet taken at another friend's wedding shower. Those pictures of Janet were the last ones taken before her death—that visit was very special to my mother.

The trial of the drunken driver, who was responsible for the accident, was conducted several months after Janet and Robert were killed. The news media repeated vivid descriptions of the fiery collision, and it carried daily accounts of the trial. Mother recalled that Joanna and some other friends were so faithful to visit throughout that painful ordeal. But many other well-meaning people avoided visiting during this time, and many of those who did visit were reluctant to talk about happy events in their own lives. Mother said she was glad for visitors who shared their joys. "We didn't begrudge anyone. Their happiness seemed to help us realize that life must go on." She explained, for instance, how uplifting it was when Joanna came by one evening to say that she and her husband were finally expecting a long-awaited baby.

Janet's first birthday after her death would have been her twenty-first birthday. Though Joanna was incredibly busy with her job, with her own family, and with making preparation for a new baby, she took time to drop in for a while. "She didn't have to explain her visit," said Mother, "we knew why she came by. Joanna never asked, 'What can I do?' She was just there."

Common Sense and Consideration

Obviously there is room for common sense and consideration in the suggestion to be there. You need, for instance, to take into account your relationship to the bereaved. While most of us genuinely grieved for the many victims of September 11, it simply was not appropriate to physically go to be with their heartbroken loved ones. Prayers, cards, financial contributions to selected agencies, etc. were the most meaningful gestures we could offer.

Generally the first twenty-four hours or so after a death is a time for family and very close friends. After that, visits by other friends and colleagues are generally comforting. Short visits can help you determine what other thoughtful gestures might help. Other friends and relatives who are available to be with the bereaved may also help you decide when your visits would help most.

Needing some time alone is a perfectly normal reaction to death and plays an important role in healing the hurt. Friends need to take this into account when planning their visits. One mother comments on this:

> Our friends gave us time to be alone, to lean on each other. This was very helpful. After Nathaniel's death I didn't want to be with anyone but my husband or family. My husband and I went out camping just to be alone with each other and our thoughts. . . . [Then] friends began to call to see how we were. This was sufficient time because our crying was pretty much over with, and we were able to talk.[35]

Friends who want to be there when needed may pick up clues from other friends and relatives, or they might simply call and ask, "Would you like for me to come over now—or in the next few days?" or "I've been thinking about you and thought you might like a phone call. Is this a good time to talk, or would you like for me to call back later?"

Even if the bereaved person asks you to come by or call later, your inquiry is generally a healing gesture in itself because it dissipates some of the loneliness. If asked to describe in one word their feelings during the first year after the death of their loved one, many grief-stricken people would respond, "Loneliness." Several years ago, in fact, when Billy Graham was asked what one problem plagues people more than any other, he, too, answered in a single word, "Loneliness."

Albert Schweitzer, the venerable medical missionary, said, "We are all so much together and yet we are all dying of loneliness." The eminent Swiss psychiatrist, Dr. Paul Tournier, called loneliness "the most devastating malady of the age."

Loneliness created by the death of a loved one is difficult to explain, for it haunts people even when many others are surrounding them. It's as though no one can fill the vacuum created by the death. The mother of C. S. Lewis died when he was a child. He described his feelings after her death:

> With my mother's death all settled happiness,
> all that was tranquil and reliable, disappeared from my
> life. There was to be much fun, many pleasures, many
> stabs of joy; but no more of the old security. It was sea
> and islands now; the great continent had sunk like
> Atlantis.[36]

Facing the Future

This loneliness is intensified, say grief experts, because of the grief-stricken's anxiety about the future without the loved one. For many, this fear of the future revolves around financial concerns; for others it may be worry about handling social obligations. For some, the fear is about rearing the children. Whatever the fears and perplexities about the future, they may be overwhelming.

The fear of the unknown is forceful. Grief-stricken people face many unknowns—the pain of grief may be the only thing they know for sure. Many, no doubt, identify with the cry of the ancient prophet Jeremiah: "My grief is beyond healing, my heart is sick within me." (Jeremiah 8:18, *Revised Standard Version*)

But one of the first steps you can take to make a healing difference is simply be there. When you take the time to be available and to be there, you will find other practical ways to help—other meaningful steps to take. You will lift the spirits of those who grieve, and they will say with Walt Whitman, "In the faces of men and women I see God."

Step 2

Talk Less, Listen More
You have one mouth and two ears.

"One month after their high school graduation, two boys in our community were killed in an accident," relates Bob Johns, pastor of my daughter's youth group. "I visited both sets of parents and we talked about the weather, their jobs, my job— everything but their sons." At moments like this, Bob always felt he should guard against intruding on the privacy and grief of the bereaved.

The Bereaved Person's Need to Talk

Then he heard a speaker from Compassionate Friends, a national organization that helps parents cope with the death of a child. "The speaker's son had died," Bob recalls, "and she said that from the very beginning no one would talk about him, nor did anyone want to listen to her talk about him. She admitted that her greatest fear was that her son's short life would go unnoticed, that memory of his existence would fade away." Suddenly Bob realized that grieving people might have a desperate need to talk about their feelings and about the deceased person.

Not long after that, Bob encountered the father of one of the boys killed in that accident. After some chitchat, Bob said, "Scott and I had such a good visit the last time I saw him." Immediately, the father's face lit up. "Really! What did you talk about?" he asked. "What did Scott say?" Remembering as much detail as he could, Bob recounted their last conversation. "Then Scott's father, in turn, started talking," says Bob, "and it was like a floodgate opening up." As Bob Johns shared this experience with me, I gained new understanding and appreciation for the wisdom expressed by the Greek philosopher, Epictetus: "Nature has given to man one tongue but two ears that we may hear from others twice as much as we speak."

Rather than following the sound course of action suggested here when it comes to talking with our grief-stricken friends, most people are more likely described by this familiar saying: "In one ear and out the other."

Many of us do not listen carefully to our friends at any time, but this is especially true when they are ravaged with fresh grief. We are too preoccupied, thinking of what we can say that will be consoling. The urge to rush in with all sorts of condolences is overwhelming. We feel compelled to say something that will help assuage the agony of grief. Our motive is noble, but our method is wrong. Rather than our doing all the talking to help heal the human spirit, we need to allow the brokenhearted to talk. One expert explains it this way:

> People are desperate for someone to listen to them. The need is especially deep during grief. The ability to simply listen is the greatest possible help in every stage of grief. During the time of shock, people

need to tell the story again and again. As reality dawns, they need someone to explain it to. When reactions begin, they need someone who will accept the stage they are in. A good listener becomes a personal intensive care unit.[1]

The Value of Listening

Bob Johns's experience and that of many others show clearly that listening to our suffering friends truly does help heal the gaping wound of grief much more readily than any persuasive words we might utter. A behavioral scientist, Elton Mayo, pointed out the value of listening this way: "One friend, one person who is truly understanding, who takes the trouble to listen to us as we consider our problems, can change our whole outlook on the world."

One man who changed the whole outlook on the world is Jesus Christ. The model he provided for a balance between talking and listening is no exception. Consider this observation:

> Father Richard Madden, abbot at the Carmelite Fathers Monastery in Youngstown, Ohio, wrote out all the words that Jesus spoke in his lifetime. Then he read them into a recorder at a normal speaking rate. He discovered that the total amount of time Jesus spoke in public was eleven minutes. What a wonderful model for our new goal to talk less and listen more![2]

A prayer entitled "Prayer to Be a Better Listener" and attributed to the Christophers of New York City may inspire us in our efforts to talk less and listen more to our bereaved friends:

We do not really listen to each other, God. Instead of true dialogue, we carry on two parallel monologues. I talk. My companion talks. But what we are really concentrating on is how to sound good, how to make our points strongly. Teach us to listen as your Son listened to everyone who spoke with him. Remind us that somehow your truth, your love, your goodness are seeking us out in the truth, love, and goodness being communicated. Teach us to be still, Lord, that we may truly hear.[3]

The Ability to Empathize

To truly hear our grieving friends requires the ability to empathize. That is, we need to "feel with" our suffering friends. We need to be able to enter mentally and emotionally into their emotions to be as aware as possible of what they are feeling. Empathy, in turn, requires truly caring about the other. The Scriptures say it this way: "Don't just pretend that you love others: really love them." (Romans 12:9, *The Living Bible*) Regardless of how we listen or what we say to our mourning friends, if we lack love and empathy, the words of the apostle Paul might as well be describing us: "If I speak in the tongues of men and of angels, but have not love, I am a noisy gong or a clanging cymbal." (First Corinthians 13:1, *Revised Standard Version*)

Determining What Is Talked About

Letting our grief-stricken friends talk about what they need and want to talk about is one of the most important ways to be an empathetic listener. In other words, we need to let our friends set the agenda to help heal their hurt. This guideline for meaningful, constructive conversation applies to other situations as well, but it is especially healing to a bereaved person. Consider, for example, the following scenario: Jan entered the house quietly. She took a basket of fresh fruit to the large family room where little groups of people were standing around, talking in hushed voices. Jan then went to Marcy, gave her a long hug and said softly, "I'm sorry."

Dan, Marcy's husband, had been returning from a long business trip late the evening before. The highway patrolmen could not piece together exactly what had happened. Evidently Dan's car had hit the median and then flipped three times. "The emergency room physician said he died instantly," Marcy said and began telling Jan all she knew about the accident. Wayne broke away from a small group upon hearing Marcy commence repeating the details. "You've talked enough about the accident. You don't need to put yourself through it again." Marcy kept right on speaking as if there had been no interruption.

Marcy is typical of many inconsolable persons in that first stunned, shocked stage. People in this stage may need to relate the details of the death over and over again. They feel compelled to repeat their story—as though they are trying to get a grip on the reality of it all. During this time they need sincerely interested and concerned listeners who can refrain from interrupting the struggling griever's comments. Concerned friends would do well to remember the wisdom expressed by Shakespeare: "Give sorrow words; the grief that does not speak whispers the o'er fraught heart and bids it break." Expressing one's grief is simply part of the coping process. A counselor who has helped numerous people cope with grief explains it this way:

> Listening can turn grief into growth. We do
> not take grief away from people—we simply help them

walk through it. The method of walking through is to talk it out. They need to talk it out to a good listener.[4]

We sometimes try to distract the grief-stricken person. We mistakenly believe we should "take their minds off" the death by talking about other completely unrelated topics. Sometimes we frantically fill the silence with meaningless chatter. Or we keep as busy as possible helping with the food or other details that require our attention. Encouraging the grief-stricken to set the agenda and express the burning emotions they are feeling at the time helps heal the hurt much more than talking about the weather, the price of oil, the latest terrorist attack, or the day's local news.

Letting the bereaved person determine what is talked about is helpful not only in the first stages of grief, but throughout the long, jolty recovery journey. This approach, ironic as it seems, provides a wellspring of courage. Talking about the death and the engulfing emotions with compassionate friends somehow enables people to "get a handle" on their grief and to face it more fearlessly.

Anne Morrow Lindbergh, wife of Charles Lindberg, noted aviator who made the first nonstop solo flight from New York to Paris in 1927, was heartbroken when their infant son was kidnapped, held hostage, and then murdered. She spoke and wrote about the long-term bravery required to face such a tragedy: "It isn't for the moment you are struck that you need courage but for the long uphill climb back to sanity and faith and security."

Ways a Listening Friend Can Help

Asking our grieving friends how they are doing or adjusting and listening gently as they tell us is another simple but helpful way of encouraging them back to "sanity and faith and security." A friend told me, for example, how heart-touching this thoughtful gesture was to her after the sudden and tragic death of her only daughter. "People who ask how I am doing give a needful boost," she says.

In contrast, some people avoid asking, thinking they should not remind the person about the death. "No need for that worry," my friend says, "for it takes a lot longer to get over deaths of loved ones than many people think. Thoughts of our dead loved ones float in and out of our consciousness for a long time." She concludes, "People who ask how I am doing and then listen with unfeigned concern to what I say help put soothing bandages on my horrible hurt."

When Husbands Die, a very insightful book by a widow, Shirley Reeser McNally, and assisted by two other widows, underscores the long-term nature of grief recovery and how a good listener can help the healing process. Numerous widows shared their stories in McNally's book, and there was a common thread. The widows wanted to tell their story, and the need to tell their story did not diminish with time. A genuinely interested listener served a significant role in each widow's grief recovery.

Realize the Need for Sensitivity

Sensitivity is required, of course, in asking grief-stricken persons how they are adjusting. A simple "I've been thinking about you; how are you doing?" is enough to let them know you care. Their answer will tell you if they want to talk more. If the place you happen to meet or be with the bereaved individual—such as the grocery store—is simply not appropriate to talk in depth and you sense that the person is uncomfortable but does want to talk more, saying something like the following may be a considerate next step:

"Why don't you give me a call this evening?"

"Give me a call whenever you need to talk."

"Would you like to have lunch next Monday so we could talk?"

Here is what one father whose child had died had to say about how helpful one friend was:

> Most of my men friends didn't know what to do or what to say. However, I had one friend who would come over and take me for a drive or a game of golf. I remember when everything was very tense and he asked me at one point, "How do you feel about it?" He wanted to know how I felt. He was not like most of the men that talked to me. When I would mention anything about the death, they would just say "fine" and go on to something else—just another piece of business to be dealt with. It helped me tremendously to have somebody who was interested and who cared enough to ask.[5]

Listening attentively but not pressing for more information than the griever wants to share is also important. After the death of her daughter, for instance, my friend said she appreciated people asking her how she was doing without pushing her for more discussion than she wanted at the moment. She admitted at times she wanted to talk more but was fearful of crying. "My emotions frequently were as fragile as a thin sheet of ice. I simply could not handle talking about Kimberly without shattering," she explained, "but my friends' asking was consoling, their taking time to listen was comforting, and their letting me change the subject was compassionate."

Friends who listen carefully can also find other practical and concrete ways to help the bereaved. We all are familiar with that feeling of wanting to help but not knowing what to do. A comment in a book on how to genuinely listen to those we care about emphasizes how keen listening can help us out: "A good listener is not only popular everywhere, but after a while he gets to know something."[6] A case in point. About three weeks after Jim died, Bonnie, his widow, was talking to several of her friends. "The practical things Jim did around the house," she commented, "are overwhelming to me—like taking care of the lawn. I can't keep on paying to have it done, but I don't know how to start the mower or the edger."

Linda had been searching for a meaningful way to help Bonnie, and now she knew the answer. Linda enjoyed lawn work and was handy with the mower and other equipment. After Linda returned home, she telephoned Bonnie and told her she would like to help her learn how to care for her lawn. Not wanting to be left out, Ben, Linda's husband, accompanied Linda the first time she went over to help Bonnie, and he still helps with some of the bigger jobs. Now Bonnie and Linda trade off and each helps the other. Says Linda, "Bonnie is so appreciative of how I met a very practical need in her life, and my own life has been enriched."

Offer Specific Encouragement

Listening carefully and openly to your friends will also undoubtedly provide you with opportunities to help calm their inner chaos and to encourage them in specific ways. Many people who have suffered the death of a loved one feel they are on a treacherous ride with a one-way ticket and will never get back to normal. They cannot sleep—or they sleep too much. They cannot concentrate—or they become obsessed with one or two concerns. They fall prey to sudden and unexplainable aches and pains and hear ringing in their ears. Their eating patterns are irregular. Their moods are mercurial, but most of the time, according to one widow, they feel like "the heavy black clouds of grief have moved in and settled low for a long, cold winter."

This same widow pointed out that most bereaved people do not want to admit "all these crazy things" to their friends, for they feel they are surely the only ones who ever felt this way. Perhaps close observation and gentle questioning will reveal areas of concern they would like to talk about. For instance, Edie commented at an appropriate moment to her newly widowed friend, "You look tired. Are you sleeping well?" At this, the friend poured out her inability to sleep—or that she would go to sleep only to wake up in the middle of the night, staying awake for hours, tossing and turning.

The Lebanese-American philosopher Kahlil Gibran offers advice on communicating with our grieving friends: "The reality of the other person is not in what he reveals to you, but in what he cannot reveal to you. Therefore, if you would understand him, listen not to what he says but rather to what he does not say."

Provide Reassurance

Bereaved individuals may be hesitant to share their real feelings because they fear unwitting reproach or put-downs. People need to accept what their grief-wracked friends tell them and treat their comments seriously.

One widower, for example, told a colleague he felt chest pains every evening about the same time his wife had died of a heart attack. Rather than saying something like, "You're probably just imagining things," the colleague insightfully responded, "I've heard that it's not unusual at all to experience the same symptoms the dead person had before dying, but to give you peace of mind, why don't you have yourself checked out."

The widower did go to a physician for an examination. The doctor also told him that stress, tension, and identifying closely with the deceased could cause the same symptoms. The widower was given a clean bill of health, and soon afterwards he reported that the pains had disappeared. This situation illustrates something I once read: "People don't need a doctor. They need an audience: just one interested listener."

Margaret provides another example of how friends who genuinely listen can provide calm reassurance. She relates how she could hardly face each day after her husband died. Her adult children were trying to persuade her to sell her large home and move closer to them. Several other relatives were coaxing her to join them in a retirement complex. All these well-meaning individuals merely wanted the best for Margaret, but, as Margaret put it, "I could hardly get out of bed each day and put one foot in front of the other, much less face a move."

Margaret said those who encouraged her and restored her confidence most successfully were those who listened to her concerns and fears and were, in turn, realistic in their comments. One friend, for instance, told her, "You'll have some good hours and some bad ones, but the good hours and days will become more and more frequent." Another friend whose daughter and grandchild had been killed in a car wreck several years before gave Margaret heart when she said, "Don't give up! Tomorrow will be a better day." A widower's comment also avoided false cheer but offered down-to-earth encouragement to Margaret: "I know you don't believe it now, but you will feel better."

After listening to Margaret for a while, another friend calmed and assured her this way: "You don't have to make a decision this very day about moving. Right now just concentrate on each hour and each day." To reinforce her encouragement, this friend gave Margaret a recording of the song, "One Day at a Time." When Margaret felt that she needed renewed reassurance, she listened to these words:

> I'm only human,
> I'm just a woman.
> Help me believe in what I could be
> and all that I am.
> Show me the stairway I have to climb.
> Lord, for my sake, teach me to take
> one day at a time.
> One day at a time, Sweet Jesus,
> That's all I'm asking from You.
> Just give me the strength to do every day
> what I have to do.
> Yesterday's gone, Sweet Jesus,
> And tomorrow may never be mine.
> Lord, help me today,
> Show me the way one day at a time.[7]

Share Memories of the Deceased

Reminiscing about the dead loved one is another effective way to help ease the choking sorrow. The funeral, of course, generally memorializes the dead person. Listening to the milestones in the life of the deceased and to his or her contributions is comforting, but talking informally about the life of this loved one offers tremendous solace. Pearl Buck once said, "How quickly, in one instant, years of happy life become only memories!" These memories can play an important part in helping heal the hurt. Sharing about the praiseworthy qualities and deeds is one of the most satisfying ways to begin recounting memories. After my father-in-law died, for example, adult children, in-laws, and grandchildren overflowed the house. "Daddy was a good man," someone said. "Yes," several agreed aloud. Then someone else offered, "Remember when . . ." And the heartfelt comments went on at length as each person shared his or her feelings and the others listened to the experiences verifying that "Daddy was a good man." Sharing and hearing these accounts was heartwarming and consoling.

When Jack was shot down in a bloody military skirmish on foreign soil, Karen's world crumbled. Some time passed before she was able to talk about her husband of twelve years without completely collapsing. Then she found herself wanting to capture forever in her memory his good qualities. Talking about Jack to other people—attentive listeners—was important to her. She found that when she talked about him, others would always add their own comments about what they admired about him. "Recalling his sterling qualities was comforting," Karen says. She notes, for example, "I found telling others Jack was proud to fight—and die—for his country and world freedom helped soften the blow of his death."

Reminiscing about my grandmother's praiseworthy virtues has been a cherished balm of Gilead for me as well as for other members of our family. Before she died, her mind was destroyed by a series of strokes, and she required around-the-clock professional care. All our family suffered at the death of Grandmother's spirit, her independence, her pride. We suffered because we knew she would prefer death to this loss of dignity. Coping with the inexpressible grief seems more manageable whenever we start reminiscing about the Grandmother we all once knew and loved. She had many splendid traits, so remembrance of them comes easily. "She had determination," one relative said at a recent family conclave. We all thought of incidents that we were personally aware of in Grandmother's long and illustrious life that would vouch for that statement.

We listened as each person in turn contributed. "Just think how her first husband died in the 1918 Spanish Flu epidemic that killed an estimated one hundred million people worldwide," one person commented. Another continued, "She had three young children and a New Mexico homestead. She sold the homestead and put the money in the bank for safekeeping. Within three months an unscrupulous banker took nearly all the bank's money and fled, and was never caught." We had all heard this story down through the years, but we listened with fresh interest to this relative's version.

"Grandmother was unwavering in her determination to keep her children together," said one of her grown children, now a grandparent herself. Someone else gave an account of how Grandmother worked literally day and night to provide for her children. Another picked up on the story and shared how Grandmother started working in a small business. As Grandmother always put it, she was "low man on the totem pole," but within a few years this *grande dame* owned the place.

One of the grandchildren then told his version of Grandmother's commitment to encourage others. "She would help anybody who wanted an education and was willing to work." Someone interjected, "How many grandchildren lived with her to attend the university in her hometown?" Everybody pitched in to come up with the impressive total. Then a grandson added, "And she provided a job in the family business for each one of them—or anyone for that matter who needed a job and was conscientious."

Now that Grandmother is freed from her age-worn body and her precious soul has entered eternity, we will still reminisce about what a remarkable person she was and how she inspired others and brought the best out of them. Many of our memories are recorded in a book entitled *Remembering Mattie: A Pioneer Woman's Legacy of Grit, Gumption, and Grace.* Her life will live on, not only in this book but also in our frequent references to her, reflecting God and a little bit of heaven, as John Greenleaf Whittier expressed in his poem:

God calls our loved ones. But we lose not
Wholly what He hath given;
They live on earth in thought and deed
as truly as in His Heaven.

Reminiscences do not have to be serious to be healing. The writer of Ecclesiastes tells us, "To every thing there is a season, and a time to every purpose under the heaven. . . . A time to weep, and a time to laugh. . . ." (Ecclesiastes 3:1, 4) During the tense times of weeping and mourning over the death of a loved one, laughter can serve as a tension breaker and a safety valve. Sensitivity, of course, is required for the right place and timing for humor. However, recollecting some of the amusing incidents shared with the deceased may be the golden touch that lightens the heavy burden of grief.

My family, for example, enjoys retelling the story of how my father-in-law and our ten-year-old Silky Terrier, Toby, enjoyed an instantaneous mutual admiration society. My husband says a dog was never allowed in the house as he was growing up. Knowing this, we always put Toby in the kennel when we visited my husband's parents. One Christmas Mrs. Chesser called us and invited us to stay a few days with them during the holidays. "By the way, bring Toby," she said, "for there's no reason that little dog cannot stay here." Well, Toby entered their front door, walked right over to Mr. Chesser, looked him in the eye as though to say, "Thanks for the invitation," and sat down at Mr. Chesser's feet. Mr. Chesser and Toby kept up a "conversation" most of the evening. When Mr. Chesser rose out of his chair to go to bed, Toby followed him, waited for him to get into bed, and then jumped on the foot of his bed. Mr. Chesser had been quite ill, wracked with pain, and had little to cheer him, but this little dog's devoted attention pleased him beyond words. That was Mr. Chesser's last Christmas in this life, and that story—silly as it may seem to outsiders—always brought a smile to my mother-in-law as well as to the rest of us.

A story my own family enjoyed for decades involved my grandfather. He was actually my step-grandfather; my mother's real father was the one who died in the Spanish Flu epidemic. My grandmother remarried several years later. Granddad recounted how at age twenty-one he was diagnosed as having terminal tuberculosis and was sent from the cold Midwest to the high, dry plains of eastern New Mexico. The doctor told him that he might as well live out his last few months as comfortably as possible. Granddad lived to be eighty-nine, enjoying life fully up until the last, and he delighted in telling just how many months he "lived out his life comfortably." This story was a favorite right after Granddad died.

Reminiscing about Granddad's sense of humor always brings a comforting chuckle in our family as each member remembers his or her own favorite incident. One incident Grandmother enjoyed telling revolves around Granddad as a consummate speller. Granddad was a walking dictionary, and I always found it easier to ask him how to spell a word than to look it up. He soon caught onto my strategy. One day he looked at me seriously and said, "I think you have a dangerous disease that will 'do you under' if you don't get rid of it." Valuing Granddad's opinion about everything, I asked intently, "What is it?" He instructed, "Get your pencil, and I will spell it for you." With pencil in hand, I began writing letter by letter as he spelled aloud: "L-A-Z-I-N-E-S-S."

The "Remember when . . ." conversations can be spirit lifting, but for some it takes longer than others to progress to this point in grief recovery. At first, for instance, Jon and LeAnne could only weep about eight-year-old Jonathan's death. They were on an outing about an hour's drive from home when he was killed. Jonathan ran into the road to catch a high-flying Frisbee. A driver watching the faraway sailboats did not see Jonathan's trim, tanned body dart in front of him. Jonathan lived about twelve hours, never fully regaining consciousness. Jon held his hand during the last hours, asking him to respond by squeezing his hand if he heard his father. Jon's last question was, "If you know we love you, squeeze my hand." Jonathan squeezed ever so slightly. He died about ten minutes later.

Jonathan's parents found reminiscing difficult, but both said when they finally came to the point where they could talk about Jonathan's short life with others and relate what they had enjoyed about it, they felt they had reached a milestone in their grief recovery. When they could chuckle with their other children and friends about some of Jonathan's boyish antics, they knew they had passed yet another constructive turning point in their healing.

Share Gratitude

Sharing expressions of gratitude can also help restore some sense of well-being to a grief-torn individual. When Marilyn was a teenager, her mother died. In spite of all the condolences offered to Marilyn, she said she felt like "a helpless feather, caught in a whirlwind." One afternoon after some especially spirit-shattering setbacks, Marilyn was spilling out her despair and loneliness caused by her mother's death. Her friend listened compassionately and then said at just the right time, "I'm so glad I knew your mother."

A fresh new feeling swept over Marilyn. She explains, "I was suddenly deeply thankful that I had had sixteen years with a terrific mother. . . . I was glad to have a friend who helped me become more aware of my appreciation and to voice it." Marilyn admitted that she had always heard, "Give thanks in all circumstances." (First Thessalonians 5:18, *Revised Standard Version*) But the healing power of gratitude, she explained, became real to her only after her mother's death.

The Double Grief of Death and Social Stigma

A suicide, a death from AIDS or from a drug overdose, or any other death or loss that creates embarrassment or social stigma brings double grief to the family. A double portion of love, in turn, is needed to heal the splintered spirits. Finding something to be thankful for at first may indeed be difficult. Initially friends need to give the survivors opportunities to vent their feelings—which may include anguish, regrets, resentment, guilt, anger, bewilderment. Friends should listen compassionately without making moral judgments, or appearing shocked, or trying to avoid the subject.

The parents of Dave say this approach helped give them life-sustaining support and courage when their oldest son died of asphyxiation after parking his car in the garage, closing the door, and turning on the motor. Dave was an outstanding student—"kind and sensitive to everyone," as one friend put it. A member of a prestigious organization on his college campus, Dave had participated in the initiation rites when a new initiate died. From that time on Dave's life was a downward spiral.

The father admitted that the first year after Dave's death was almost unbearable. "Our boy was born on Valentine's Day, 1958. We truly felt he was a gift of love, and he always had a love for his family and for others. Perhaps he was too sensitive and loved too much for his own good. After the student died in the college initiation, Dave just could not pull himself together. He felt so responsible." Then the father went on to say, "I remember once when we were talking about that awful accident that he said he'd give anything if he could trade his life for that boy's. . . ."

"Friends were so kind to us," says the mother. "They truly showed us God's love and compassion. We felt a renewed acceptance of life when we were able—with the help of God and our friends—to dwell not on Dave's tragic death but on all the goodness in his life." The capacity of these distraught parents to survive the loss of their beloved son was enhanced by caring friends—good listeners who gently shared happy memories.

Actions That Hurt Rather Than Help

Leo Buscaglia says in *Living, Loving and Learning* that our prime purpose in life is to help others. Next, he makes the point, "If you can't help them at least don't hurt them."[8] When someone dies, friends and relatives generally want to help, but sometimes they hurt instead. By knowing some of the actions that can be hurtful, perhaps we will be able to avoid hurting our friends when the sunlight has gone out of their life and they stand alone in the darkness of grief. We may not always be able to help them, but at least we won't hurt them.

Doing or Saying Nothing

One of the most distressful things for the bereaved is for a friend to do or say nothing. Oftentimes because people fear hurting their grieving friend, they are afraid to do anything—they are simply paralyzed or immobilized. Nevertheless, from the heartbroken person's perspective, they are getting "the silent treatment," and this hurts deeply. George Bernard Shaw, a noted British dramatist, expressed this notion in these words: "The worst sin towards our fellow creatures is not to hate them, but to be indifferent to them; that's the essence of inhumanity."[9]

Saying the Wrong Thing

Saying the wrong thing can also cause pain. People mean well, but they are often uncomfortable or nervous. Feeling compelled to say something, they sometimes say hurtful things. Bereaved persons, for example, are not helped by comments like the following:

> "Don't cry."
> "Be brave."
> "You'll get over it."
> "You shouldn't feel that way."
> "Pull yourself together."
> "Come on, get hold of yourself."
> "No use crying. The past is the past."

Adults sometimes put heavy demands on children by making awful comments like these:

> "Be a good little girl and don't cry."
> "Be a brave little man and don't cry."

Bereavement experts, as we have already discussed, emphasize the importance of resolving grief—regardless of age—rather than denying it or repressing it. So we must avoid saying anything that would discourage our friends from expressing their grief. As one widower put it, "I need to get it out of my system." Doug Manning supports this idea throughout his insightful book, *Don't Take My Grief Away*. He suggests saying something like this: "You have a thousand whys—ask them all" or "You have a million feelings—feel them all."[10] Comments like these may help: "I know you are hurting—it's only natural to cry," or "Go ahead and cry—I'll cry with you." A simple comment like this may also be appropriate: "It's okay to cry—you loved her a lot."

Experts (and grieving persons, who are experts in their own

rights!) also contend that statements with the essence of "It could've been worse . . ." offer little consolation. A young couple, for instance, who had a difficult pregnancy, finally lost the baby at seven months. Some well-meaning person offered, "It [the baby] would probably have been deformed." The mother's comment was, "That was supposed to be consoling? I cried all evening." A similar statement people sometimes offer when a baby is stillborn is equally hurtful: "Something probably would've been wrong with it." Parents also say referring to the dead baby as "it" is hurtful and should be avoided. Simply saying "the baby" or "he" or "she" is much kinder.

In *The Survival Guide for Widows*, Betty Jane Wylie describes this "It could've been worse" approach after her husband died:

> I have one friend who, whenever we got together, at one point would nod her head wisely and say sententiously, "There are worse things than death." It was home-truth time, and she wanted me to know how lucky I was that I didn't have a living vegetable tied up to tubes in the hospital, or a human skeleton wasting away with pain in front of my eyes. I know, I know. We are given enough strength, I hope, to bear our own pain. I would not trade with others, nor they with me, in all likelihood. . . . But the widow doesn't feel very lucky and resents being reminded that she still owes a debt of gratitude. She'll come around to it.[11]

Also avoid comments like the following:

> "Be glad your marriage was ended by death and not by divorce."
> "At least he's out of his misery."

"Be glad it wasn't one of your children."

"Losing your husband this young should make it easier to adjust."

Mary Brite reports in her book, *Triumph Over Tears*, these comments which widows found hurtful:

"You must go on for the sake of your children."

"Shape up. You probably would have had terrible problems with each other by the time the kids were teenagers."

"Most of us become widows at some time. You're just one sooner."[12]

Telling Hard-luck Stories

Likewise, hard-luck stories do not help heal the hurt. Some people think sharing disastrous tales with the bereaved will help soften the blow they have just experienced. Not so. Right after Janet and Robert were killed by the drunk driver, for instance, various people wanted to share detailed accounts of other tragedies caused by drunk drivers. We realized our family was not the only one stricken by this appalling national epidemic, but handling our own personal grief was difficult enough, especially right at first. The gruesome details of losses suffered by others did not help heal our hurt.

Suggesting the Replacement of the Dead Loved One

Compassionate people also sometimes think it helps a grieving person to concentrate on the prospect of replacing the dead loved one. It does not help, say mourning people—not when fresh grief is such a painful reminder of the irreplaceable nature of bonds that have been severed forever. So comments like these are neither helpful nor healing:

>"You'll get married again."
>
>"You're lucky to be young enough to have other children."
>
>"Are you going to try to have another baby?"
>
>"Time will heal."
>
>"You'll get over it."
>
>"You are young and nice-looking. You will get married again."

Saying, "I know how you feel"

Heartbroken people also say that the well-intentioned comment, "I know how you feel" is not helpful unless the person has experienced an almost identical loss. More healing comments might be "I know you're hurting. I'll be praying for you." Or "We loved her too. We'll be thinking about you during these days."

Giving Advice

Another well-meaning but often hurtful attempt at helping the grief-stricken is giving them advice. Everyone wants to be helpful, and people often feel certain they know what is best for their grieving friends. Shakespeare observed this characteristic of human nature long ago when he said, "Everyone can master a grief but he who has it." Mark Twain also commented on this common human frailty by saying something like, "I can handle any kind of adversity—as long as it is not mine."

One newly-widowed individual made this observation:

"Everybody was telling me what to do or what not to do. One would say, 'Clear Jake's study out,' and the next would say, 'Leave things as they are for a while.' I felt like some of my friends' feelings were hurt when I didn't follow their advice. This added to my confusion and frustration. Also with everyone giving me advice, I had no confidence in my own ability to know what was the right thing for me to do."

People whose lives have been stripped of security and predictability and confidence—whose life's course of action has been drastically altered—can easily identify with the words of the psalmist: ". . . my eye is wasted from grief, my soul and my body also. For my life is spent with sorrow." (Psalm 31: 9-10, *Revised Standard Version*)

Bereaved people face what Dag Hammarskjöld called "the longest journey, the journey inward."[13] Even though we may be certain we know the very best way for our grieving friends to make this "journey," we should withhold our "wisdom." Consider what one widow suggests:

> Don't give her unsolicited advice. Don't tell her what to do. Don't make harsh judgments of what she has done. She's supersensitive anyway. If she wants your advice, she'll ask for it.[14]

Another widow's observation about advice included these words: ". . . the disturbing remarks, advice, and suggestions that penetrated our deep shock and sounded like crashing cymbals when our nerves demanded a soft touch."[15]

This widow's attitude is similar to that of many grief-stricken people: she simply had the courage to voice it while others may not. Her comments remind me of the definition of advice given in a whimsical little volume called *The Devil's Dictionary*: ADVICE—the smallest current coin.[16]

A psychologist, the late Haim Ginott, also placed little value on advice. He said, "I avoid telling [others] what to do and what not to do. Even when they ask for it, I postpone giving instant advice. I try to find out what they think about the situation and what alternatives they have considered. I encourage them to talk about their fears and hopes and to risk stating opinions and making decisions."[17]

A situation in which Dr. Ginott's philosophy worked well involved Max, whose wife died after an extended illness. "Some friends were encouraging me to take the promotion my boss had offered and transfer to another city," says Max, "and some were insisting that I move to a condominium across town. Others were 'absolutely sure' I should do this or that." Max goes on to say, "Looking back, I can see how one friend helped me a lot. He let me talk about the different possibilities and what others were telling me I should do. At just the right time, he'd ask something like, 'What have you considered doing?' or 'How do you feel about it?'"

"Another friend who helped me decide what was best for me," says Max, "is one who discouraged me from making any important, far-reaching decisions." Max remembers the friend saying something like this, "I've heard that it's best not to make any major decisions for at least a year after a loved one dies. What do you think about 'staying put' for a while? Then perhaps you can reconsider what's best for you."

By following the example set by Max's friends and Dr. Ginott, perhaps we can avoid hurting our bereaved friends. A grief counselor put it this way:

> If you want to heal people, learn to "lay ears" on them. People must solve their own problems. We cannot do it for them. We cannot work out their thinking or their feelings because it is impossible for us to know what [they are] really thinking or feeling in the depth of their souls. But we can give

them the ingredient needed to work problems out for themselves, by listening while they talk.[18]

Shakespeare's advice on advice giving was brief and to the point: "Give every man thine ear but few thy voice" and "Reserve thy judgment."

Repeating Pat Answers and Pious Platitudes

If we truly listen to our grief-stricken friends, sooner or later they may bring up the question of "Why?" Mortimer Alder called this "The Great Conversation" and pointed out that it has been going on for centuries as men and women have searched for the reason why there are tragedies, suffering, and death in this life. A number of excellent books have been written exploring this issue in depth, including *When Bad Things Happen to Good People*; *Why Us? When Bad Things Happen to God's People*; *God in the Hard Times*; and *If God Cares, Why Do I Still Have Problems?* The authors of these books conclude what Eugenia Price states in the title of her book, *No Pat Answers*.

No philosophic answers satisfactorily explain the "why" of hurt and tragedy. Feeling compelled to try though, our explanations usually are designed to defend God. We say things like, "It was God's will," or "There must be some reason for this," or "It's for the best."

These simplistic pious platitudes are rarely comforting, say the experts and people who have endured the death of a loved one. A college student, for example, vividly remembers receiving no solace from several sincere people who said something like, "Your father is in heaven now" and "God knows best." Most people do depend on their religious beliefs for strength at the time of a death, but bereaved persons need to work this out within the context of their own religious beliefs, in their own recovery process, and in their own timing. Others bombarding them with religious truisms soon after the death of a loved one is more harmful than helpful. A pastor speaking on grief put it succinctly: "Cut the clichés." I might add, remember the value of a listening spirit. When the bereaved ask the unanswerable "Why?" listening out of a caring heart is a more helpful step or approach than trying to answer the unanswerable "Why?"

Judge Abner McCall, long-time president of Baylor University, had an extensive personal acquaintance with grief. When he was three, his father died. Several years later his mother's health collapsed, and he had to be put in an orphanage where he grew up. Through the years a brother and a sister died. His first wife died. His son-in-law was killed. And his seven-year-old grandson died of leukemia. Out of his experience, Judge McCall also concluded that there are no pat answers. Here is how he put it: "It's better not to try to 'reason it out.' We simply must remember that God made us mortal, and we are all going to die sooner or later." He added, "Sometimes loved ones die sooner than we think they should and in ways we don't prefer."

When the grief-stricken ask "Why?" Judge McCall suggested saying something like: "I am sorry. I don't understand why this had to happen. I just know that God loves us and will see us through it."

In *Caring Enough to Hear*, David Augsburger emphasizes that the more deeply submerged the hope, and the more frozen the grief, the more open and caring the listening friend must be. In addition, caring means accepting what the person is feeling without judging and without trying to give pat answers. Here is how the author said it:

> In caring-hearing, the hurt is opened, the festering bitterness of resentful illusions, the burning of angry demands, the numb frozenness of grief, the staleness of depression are allowed to drain. The light is allowed to pour in, sterilizing the infections

and stimulating cells of hope and trust to begin new growth.[19]

The "Whys" may be especially piercing at the death of a baby or young person. In *Death of a Dream*, a book about the grief caused by a miscarriage, stillbirth, or death of a newborn baby, authors Donna and Rodger Ewy also suggest avoiding "canned," pat answers. They offer, instead, some sample statements that can be easily adapted for comforting those who grieve the death of a loved one of any age:

> "It is natural to feel anger and hostility toward everyone and everything that had to do with your baby's death. I feel angry too."
>
> "You must be very angry that your baby has suffered, and you can do nothing about it."
>
> "It is normal and reasonable to be angry and resentful when you have lost your baby, and others have live and healthy babies."
>
> "You have lost your baby and you have a right to be angry and frustrated."
>
> "It must be hard to find the words to express your anger, helplessness, and frustration."
>
> "It is important that you allow yourself to express your anger and rage no matter how much others try to discourage you."[20]

Offer Promises

Helen Keller, American author and lecturer who lost both her sight and hearing when she was nineteen months old, made an observation that went something like this: "Although the world is full of suffering, it is full also of promises for overcoming it." One of the best ways to help our friends overcome their suffering is to offer them promises, not advice, simplistic explanations, or clichés. Some of the most reliable promises are those offered in the bestseller that continues to meet human hunger for hope and peace—that is, the Bible. Here are some of its promises that down through the ages have provided healing:

> "The eternal God is your Refuge, and underneath are the everlasting arms." (Deuteronomy 33:27, *The Living Bible*)
>
> "When you go through deep waters and great trouble, I will be with you. When you go through rivers of difficulty, you will not drown! When you walk through the fire of oppression, you will not be burned up—the flames will not consume you. For I am the Lord your God, your Savior, the Holy One of Israel. . . . Don't be afraid, for I am with you." (Isaiah 43:2, 3, 5, *The Living Bible*)
>
> "Let not your heart be troubled: ye believe in God. . . . " (John 14:1)
>
> "For I am persuaded, that neither death, nor life, nor angels, nor principalities, nor powers, nor things present, nor things to come, nor height, nor depth, nor any other creature, shall be able to separate us from the love of God, which is in Christ Jesus our Lord." (Romans 8:38-39)
>
> "Even though I walk through the valley of the shadow of death, I fear no evil; for Thou art with me; Thy rod and Thy staff, they comfort me." (Psalm 23:4, *New American Standard Bible*)

We can share with our friends the assurance that depending on God's Word will provide "the peace of God, which passes all understanding." (Philippians 4:7, *Revised Standard Version*)

Ask How You Can Help

Simply asking the bereaved what we can do to help comfort them may be the most effective approach. They may be able to tell us how to help them. Consider, for instance, the following situation:

> As Nancy's best friend, I knew how much she wanted that baby and how devastated she must be by the death. I called Bob and told him that whenever she was ready I would come to see her. At the same time I thought I don't think I can go because I don't know what to say and there's nothing I can do. When Bob finally told me to come over, I spent half an hour trying to get up enough courage to go and see her. When I got there, the funny thing was Nancy comforted me. She told me that it was all right to cry. And so we cried together for a while. Then she told me that it was all right not to be able to say anything. Moreover, I actually came away feeling better than when I went down. After that, I kept in touch with her. I would call her and say, "I don't know what to do. I want to do something for you." Then she would tell me, "Well, this is what I need today!" We were good friends before it happened, but I think it made us a lot closer having gone through it together. We can talk about anything now.[21]

Tom also found that merely asking what you can do is a natural way to express your concern and to find out how to help comfort those who grieve. Several months after Don's wife died, Tom sensed that Don was not quite up to par. "I don't want to pry where you don't want me to," Tom said to Don one day in the privacy of Don's office, "but I feel that you are still struggling with Joan's death."

"Yeah, it's been tough," Don replied. Tom responded, "My brother's wife died a couple of years ago, so I know it takes a lot of adjusting." Then Tom offered, "I would really like to help you. Is there some specific way I can help?"

Don thought a moment. The silence did not bother either Don or Tom. "My teenage daughter has taken this awfully hard," related Don. "She and her mother were close. She and I just can't seem to talk like I wish we could." Tom said, "My wife, Karen, understands teenage girls. How about her calling your daughter sometime to take her to lunch before school starts?" Don hesitated, "Patti might feel awkward. No, she already feels awkward, so it sure wouldn't hurt anything."

Karen did call Patti, and Patti was very grateful for Karen's caring and concern. The two not only had some good sharing over lunch, but a positive relationship is still developing. Patti helps Karen with a church group of teenage girls, and she occasionally drops in at Tom and Karen's to watch television and merely chat. Karen has helped fill the vacuum in Patti's life, and Patti has helped fill a void in Tom and Karen's life since both of their daughters are married and live in different towns.

Asking specifically what you can do to help heal the hurt will not always turn out so well, but like Don put it, your offer "sure wouldn't hurt anything." And it just might be a tremendous help.

All of us generally feel inadequate to help heal the hurt of a deathblow, and we all long to be able to speak those magic words that will dissolve the pain. If we can put into practice this simple verse, "Be still and know that I am God," (Psalm 46:10) perhaps, like Don and Nancy's friends, we will sense the right thing to do. In addition, for the most part, being still and listening is the right thing to do. One communication expert put it bluntly: "Don't just stand there—Listen!"[22] And the Bible says it this way: " . . . it is best to listen much, speak little. . . ." (James 1:19, *The Living Bible*)

All the foregoing examples of the power of listening underscore the power of listening to help people cope with yet another type of grief—that suffered at the death of a pet. I would never want to minimize the heartbreak of losing a loved one, but neither would I want to omit a discussion of helping someone cope with the death of a beloved pet. I have always loved animals and suffered deeply when one of my pets died. The scene of the car running over my pet dog when I was six years old is clearly etched in my memories, and the heart-stabbing hurt is also clearly and painfully recalled. My grief over the death of a pet did not diminish during adulthood. When our eleven-year-old family mascot, Toby—a scrappy little Silky Terrier dog—met a fate like my first pet, I cried for a week. When our family cat, Mork—a beautiful, lovable, longhaired white cat larger than Toby—strangely disappeared, I began the horrendous grief process all over again. Throughout my tears, I vowed never to own another pet. I wanted to avoid subjecting myself to the anguish at the possible loss of another pet.

Then came along Mandi, an adorable black and white Lhasa Apso who instantly made me forget the serious vow I had made. It was love at first sight. The affection for Mandi only grew greater, and she was a constant companion for nearly sixteen years. She was the epitome of the perfect pet. She adored me, waited for me at the back door every day after work, listened with rapt attention to every word I spoke to her, accepted me with unconditional love in spite of my own shortcomings, etc. The amazing thing was that my husband and our daughter shared these same feelings for Mandi. We nursed Mandi through several illnesses and one major surgery for breast cancer. Her ups and downs were our ups and downs. Mandi was a family member in the truest sense.

Marla, the vet that cared for Mandi her entire lifetime, was extremely perceptive about the relationship between animals and their owners. She explained to me that some people regard their pets as animals while others regard their pets as family members. She noted early in our association with her that Mandi was a family member. When it was apparent that Mandi's long and wonderfully satisfying life was about to come to an end, Marla discussed with me how many of the owners of animals she cared for suffered tremendous pain at their death. Ways to help these grieving pet owners were strikingly similar to ways that help people handle grief over the loss of loved ones.

Children may need special attention when a family pet dies. Making us all sad was the recent death of Brando, the one-hundred-pounds-plus Italian Mastiff my son-in-law, Michael, and the rest of the family had cherished for nine years. But Ava, our three-year-old granddaughter, seemed especially affected. She had never known life without Brando. She had used him for a warm, over-sized pillow and as a companion as she watched her favorite TV programs, listened to family discussions, etc. She and her older brother were at school when Brando died. Michael and Christi (my daughter) stayed with Brando and dealt with the own grief until friends who had offered to care for the children brought them home. Then as a family they buried Brando; both parents talked about Brando, his life, his death, and answered their children's questions. Ava continued asking questions, struggling to come to grips with Brando's death. A book called *When a Pet Dies*, by Fred Rogers (the legendary Mr. Rogers, host of a children's longstanding, all-time favorite TV program) has been invaluable in answering some of Ava's questions and helping her work through her grief. Ava's reaction to death was similar to that of people of all ages—to pets and to people. She genuinely needed to talk about Brando, and she needed someone to listen to her comments and try to answer her questions.

One of my cousins, affectionately called Norcie, is no stranger to death and grief. Like many people, she treasures her pets—most frequently fiesty little West Highland Terriers. Norcie admittedly suffers deeply when one dies. In the early stages of her training and education as a registered nurse, Norcie became painfully aware of the intense emotions experienced at the death of a loved one. Then her personal life unfortunately provided further experience with death. She was only thirty-two when her husband died. Their children were eight and five. Next to die was her father—whom she dearly loved. Then the husband of her only sister died after a two-year struggle with cancer. Norcie's longtime companion, Michael, died suddenly from an aneurysm.

About halfway through these losses, Norcie served in the Persian Gulf War and saw additional deaths at their worst. Now a retired lieutenant colonel, Norcie does volunteer work, putting to good use all that she has learned about handling loss and grief. Most recently she served as a volunteer to help victims of the devastating hurricane Ike. When I asked Norcie what she considers most helpful to her as she handled her own grief as well as to those she has helped over the years, she gave a brief answer. Whatever the loss, a dear loved one, a cherished pet, a marriage, a job, a house and personal possessions etc., I believe my cousin's answer sums up an important step to help others handle grief—"Talk less, listen more."

Step 3

Attend the Service
Nobody likes funerals, but . . .

*F*ran Philips was a real estate agent for a hard-working realtor. Her boss, Helen, put in long hours and demanded the same from her sales force. During an especially busy period, Fran's mother died. Fran dreaded telling Helen. Fran's mother had lived three hundred miles away, and Fran would have to be gone several days—including the weekend, the busiest time for anyone in real estate. Fran also had several house deals that were at a critical stage of negotiation. This meant that Helen would have to handle them on top of all her other work while Fran was gone.

But Helen was warmly sympathetic. She insisted that Fran leave right away. It was winter, and heavy snows were forecast. "If you hurry," Helen said, "you might beat the weather." Two days later, at a Saturday morning service Fran was greeting her mother's friends when someone came up quietly behind her. It was Helen. She and her husband had driven all the previous night through snow. For a moment, Fran just stood there, speechless. Helen smiled. "Why stay at home," she asked, "when all my thoughts were here with you?"

When we attend a funeral or memorial service, we are saying to the surviving loved ones by our presence, "I care about you and your loss." This is how Mike Toby, a minister who has pastored churches in Florida and Texas, explains the importance of going to the service. Down through the ages ceremonies or rituals have helped people through turning points in their lives—birth, marriage, educational milestones, political and military events, as well as death. Moreover, as social psychologists would put it, friends who attend a funeral give the survivors emotional support or group support at this most significant rite of passage.

Our presence at the service is also a way of saying that the death doesn't go unnoticed. As Pastor Toby points out, it says to the family members, "I cared about the deceased." And that helps comfort the grief-stricken. Chuck Grayson, an insurance man in Lexington, Kentucky, for example, is fully convinced that people attending the service have a positive impact on the bereaved. "Before Pat, my wife, died," he explains, "I didn't go to many funerals. I didn't think it made much difference whether I went or not." He continues, "But then I saw how many friends and relatives made a special effort to be at Pat's funeral, and suddenly I saw how important this is to the person who's suffered the loss." Chuck's cousin, for example, made a two-hour drive with her baby. She also brought along her grandmother as a babysitter during the service. "Now that," says Chuck, "took some planning, and it meant a lot to me." Concludes Chuck, "Paying your last respects takes on new meaning when it's your own loved one's funeral."

A child whose father was killed provides another example of how family members genuinely appreciate those who participate in this age-old and purposeful rite. Stephen Jayne was eight when his father was killed. Mr. Jayne was a producer for ABC News, and he was on a small chartered plane going from Jordan to Beirut when it crashed, claiming the lives of all four aboard. As a young boy, Stephen had this to say about friends attending his father's funeral:

> We had a funeral in our church and all the benches were taken up and people even had to stand. So I knew my dad was important to other people. It made me feel good knowing that my parents had lots of friends.[1]

Comfort from Public Tributes

Danny Truitt also says that friends who attended the memorial service for his father helped soften the deathblow. "People who came to the service," elaborates Danny, "made me feel like they cared about me—and my father." He continues, "My father was a compassionate, generous man. It gave me, my mother, and my sister strength to see friends gathered together, listening to the pastor publicly acknowledge my father's expressions of heartfelt interest in others—how he served on the hospital visitation ministry, even after he learned of his own illness and that it was terminal . . . how he donated his body to medical science . . . how he unselfishly gave his life to God and others."

"I knew my father was a godly man," says Danny, "and hearing this fact openly stated with specific examples for all our friends to hear was not only a tribute to Dad but a tremendous consolation to me."

When the death has been particularly tragic, as in the case of a suicide, loved ones need affirmation of the person's life even more desperately. A case in point. Ashley had a beautiful oil portrait of herself made for her mother as a Christmas gift. Some time later she methodically gave away her prized possessions. At lunch break during a school day, she made her final plans—then shot herself. Ashley was buried on her sixteenth birthday. She had been a delight to all who had known her, and her suicide devastated everyone. Ashley's parents were understandably disconsolate. Rather than concentrating on her manner of death, however, friends and clergy who were helpful and comforting talked about her life. Words written for Ashley's service provide a model for friends who want to help heal the impenetrable hurt of the deathblow by affirming the life of the deceased:

> We come today to celebrate the sixteen years that Ashley lived upon this earth and also to celebrate the assurance that she is now at peace with the Lord. . .
>
> Ashley had a unique and charming sense of humor whether in her home as the youngest of four children, or out among her friends. It's hard to say the word Ashley without a smile coming across your lips. She was a master prankster. She knew how to have fun, to laugh, to cut up, to joke. Who else has taught a chicken to ride the handlebars of a bicycle, walked a coon on a leash, or painted a chicken's toenails? Cousins remember at Christmas and Thanksgiving the children's table in the kitchen behind swinging doors separating the grownups in their more formal atmosphere. Ashley's antics at the children's table added unexpected pleasure among the cousins, though often unappreciated momentarily by the adults who preferred more order.
>
> Ashley was compassionate. She gathered friends like the ocean gathers sand. Her friends range from very young children to an eighty-five-year-old cherished friend of hers. She was a champion for the

underdog, the loser, the wounded, the broken in spirit, whether animal or human. Through the sixteen years we had her, she raised literally hundreds of stray dogs, abandoned cats, crippled birds, and wounded animals. It is no wonder that the red heart is her symbol. Her compassion for the world and its seemingly unsolvable problems caused her much pain. As an example, Ashley once adopted a friend in a nursing home and spent all her allowance to be sure the elderly friend had several brightly colored packages on Christmas morning. Ashley rushed to the nursing home that morning before she opened her own presents.

Ashley was an achiever, though she chose her own areas in which to achieve. She loved her girls' softball as her many trophies will attest. She played catcher for many years, having a strong enough arm to throw a runner out at second.

Ashley was a lover of nature. The outdoors was her domain. She loved the beauty of the sunset, a starry night, the unexpected rain. Surely, as she enters heaven, she is not nearly as impressed by the streets of gold, as with the clouds, the rolling hills, the rippling streams.

And so now Ashley's sixteen years, so full for so short a time, end, and a better life begins. When Ashley was quite young, her mother led her to a personal knowledge of Jesus Christ. Ashley was so excited, she jumped on her bicycle to go share the good news with her pastor. Surely, that same excitement is present today as she goes rushing into the pearly gates, breathless, excited, and probably with her halo on slightly crooked to begin her eternal reward.[2]

At the death of a loved one, the survivors reassess everything: religious beliefs, values, relationships with other loved ones and friends, disappointments from the past, hopes for the future. Death leaves the grief-stricken the most vulnerable they will ever be. They need reassurance that the life of the dead person was significant. A good example of this involves J. Carroll Chadwick, twice-elected leader of the largest Protestant group in Texas. He had for over thirty years preached kindness, compassion, concern, and caring for each other. Martha Lou Scott, a daughter of this revered pastor, contends that the service for her father and the other related activities, like the meals and visiting, reflected the values her beloved father and spiritual mentor had taught. Not only did the officiating clergy recall the myriad ways Mr. Chadwick lived out by example the values he taught to others, the many friends and relatives reminisced about ways he had ministered to them. Martha Lou says hearing these conversations in the gatherings related to her father's death offered inestimable comfort.

Affirmation of Faith

Grief-stricken people also need renewed affirmation about eternity and how the deceased person fits into the scheme of things. Martha Lou describes how her father's funeral provided an opportunity for friends of her father to create a bond of love, a spirit of common concern, a supportive community of witnesses to the declaration of beliefs. This was all truly comforting to her, her mother, and the other loved ones. The following are some hallmark passages of Scripture which were read aloud at her father's funeral. These verses have been proclaimed at funerals down through the ages to help reinforce the faith of mourners and console them:

"Let not your heart be troubled; ye believe in God, believe also in me. In my Father's house are many mansions: if it were not so, I would have told you. I go to prepare a place for you. And if I go and prepare a place for you, I will come again, and receive you unto myself; that where I am, there ye may be also." (John 14:1–3)

"Lo! I tell you a mystery. We shall not all sleep, but we shall all be changed, in a moment, in the twinkling of an eye, at the last trumpet. For the trumpet will sound, and the dead will be raised. . . . " (First Corinthians 15:51–52, *Revised Standard Version*)

"But this I call to mind, and therefore I have hope: The steadfast love of the Lord never ceases, his mercies never come to an end; they are new every morning; great is thy faithfulness. 'The Lord is my portion,' says my soul, 'therefore I will hope in him.'" (Lamentations 3:21–24, *Revised Standard Version*)

"And I saw a new heaven and a new earth: for the first heaven and the first earth were passed away. . . . And I heard a great voice out of heaven saying, Behold . . . God shall wipe away all tears from their eyes; and there shall be no more death, neither sorrow, nor crying, neither shall there be any more pain: the former things are passed away." (Revelation 21:1, 3–4)

The Wisdom of Poets

Wisdom from great people—poets, philosophers, and others—also helps heal the hurt as friends, gathered at a service, listen conjointly. The noted journalist, John Gunther, wrote a book about the untimely death of his son, calling it *Death Be Not Proud* (no doubt the phrase came from the "Holy Sonnets X," by John Donne, an early seventeenth-century English poet). The family of one of my friends who died had passages of *Death Be Not Proud* and phrases from Donne's poem read at Stan's funeral. These words all seemed fitting to commemorate Stan's life, and the family members later said listening to them with all Stan's friends was comforting. Stan's wife said the most meaningful passage read at the funeral is one branded indelibly on her mind—and her heart:

> Death, be not proud . . .
> One short sleep past, we wake eternally
> And death shall be no more;
> Death, thou shalt die.[3]

Other observations about death that have assuaged the grief of mourners down through the ages are summed up by a short but powerful phrase attributed to St. Bernard of Clairvaux: "Death, the gate of life."

The translation from the German Aerzte-Kalender's wisdom elaborated upon this theme, and it gave solace to a young woman who was dying of cystic fibrosis. These words in turn were repeated at her funeral and provided much needed comfort to her parents and twelve-year-old brother:

> The thought of death leaves me completely calm because I have the firm conviction that our spirit is a being of an indestructible nature, continuing from eternity it is similar to the sun, which seems to set each night for us mortals, but which actually never sets,

instead continues to shine uninterruptedly.

John's wife died a torturous death from a terminal disease. He said a thought expressed by Nathaniel Hawthorne, an American novelist and short story writer, was especially meaningful to him when the pastor included it in his comments at Sara's funeral: "We sometimes congratulate ourselves at the moment of waking from a troubled dream; it may be so the moment after death."

Carrie admits that she does not remember much that was said at her husband's funeral though she felt bolstered by the many friends and relatives who were there. One of those attentive friends jotted down some of the speaker's ideas and later shared them with Carrie. "The most beautiful thought," says Carrie, "was captured by some words spoken to me and all my friends and relatives at Neal's funeral." These were those words: "Death is the opening of a more subtle life. In the flower, it sets free the perfume; in the chrysalis, the butterfly; in the man, the soul."

Words of Benjamin Franklin, the kind-faced American statesman, scientist, inventor, and writer, were shared at my grandfather's funeral. Listening to this thought with friends and relatives lessened the misery I felt at the death of one of my favorite loved ones: "Life is a state of embryo, a preparation for life. A man is not completely born until he has passed through death."

In summary, thoughts shared with family members and witnessed by friends at the funeral provide encouragement and comfort. A Roman poet, Sextus Aurelius Propertius, who lived about the same time as Christ, capsulized the innumerable quotations and passages which have sustained mourners and inspired hope down through the ages:

> There is something beyond the grave;
> death does not end it all.

Public Acknowledgment of Death

The words spoken at funerals are not only a public avowal of beliefs meant to console, but they also serve another important role in the grief process. They constitute a public pronouncement that the death has occurred. "I can't believe she (or he) is really dead," is a frequent reaction to death. A funeral helps break through that shock and disbelief, and those in attendance are witnesses to this open acknowledgment of the death. The presence of friends at this ceremony lends strength and solidarity as they come together in oneness of spirit.

Tom and Marceille Hollingsworth shared how a funeral helped them face the reality of their son's death. Tommy, their only child, graduated from the Baptist seminary in Fort Worth. He planned to go to the mission field upon completion of his doctoral studies. Because his work was in biblical languages, especially Hebrew, Tommy hoped to serve in the Middle East. He had grown up in Argentina where his parents served thirty-three years as missionaries. Just for the summer he was selling copies of the Bible in Alabama for Southwestern Publishing Company. His parents were on furlough in the United States; his father was recuperating from a massive heart attack. Two days before Mrs. Hollingsworth's birthday Tommy called her. "We had a wonderful visit," she recalls. Three days later a telephone call informed the Hollingsworths that Tommy was missing. He had failed to show up for staff meeting on Monday morning, and nobody could find any trace of him. The distraught parents knew something was terribly wrong, for Tommy had always let them know of his whereabouts. The girl Tommy was unofficially engaged to was at the Christian encampment in Glorieta, New Mexico. As soon as she was notified, she came home. The parents assisted the police in the investigation and search. For nine agonizing days they all worked, waited, hoped, and prayed.

When the officials called to relay the tragic news that Tommy had been murdered, Mr. Hollingsworth turned to his wife and said, "We don't have to worry about Tommy anymore. He is at home with the Lord."

As the mystery of the murder unraveled, it appeared that two young men had tried to rob Tommy. But what started out as a robbery turned into a brutal murder. Tommy's body was found flung onto an open field. His personal belongings were strewn about. His car was nearby, doors open. His personal copy of the Bible was lying open on the ground near him. A search was begun in the small town, Alexander City, Alabama. An elderly lady recognized Tommy's face on the television as the courteous young man who had visited her home, asking her if she would like to buy a Bible. Somehow she suspected her grandson of the murder, so she called the police. Sure enough, her grandson and one of his friends who needed money to support their drug habit had carried out the heinous crime.

The funeral for Tommy Hollingsworth helped shatter the shock of his death. Friends came from afar to be with the Hollingsworths to help them face the fact of their son's death and to pay tribute to the exemplary life he had lived. Mrs. Hollingsworth recounts how her son's funeral brought back memories of other deaths in her life. She had been married only a few months when World War II broke out. Her first husband was sent to the South Pacific, where he was killed shortly after his arrival. He was buried at sea. In addition, her mother—whom she loved dearly—had died at an early age. This funeral for her beloved son was an insufferable reminder that death comes to all sooner or later—and that reality is the beginning of grief recovery. But the funeral was also a celebration of the Hollingsworths' belief in God, in God's goodness, and in God's power to comfort, as expressed in Second Corinthians 1:3: "Blessed be God . . . the Father of mercies, and the God of all comfort."

The funeral also was a celebration of Tommy's spiritual life. "He had been a wonderful son," says Mr. Hollingsworth, "and he genuinely tried to be what the Lord meant him to be." John Claypool, a personal friend of the Hollingsworths, officiated at the funeral. Claypool's own young daughter had died of leukemia; he described this grief journey in *Tracks of a Fellow Struggler*. "This dear friend," says Mr. Hollingsworth, "made Tommy's funeral what it needed to be to give us comfort as well as courage to face his physical death." John Claypool reminded the Hollingsworths and all their friends and relatives that Tommy was celebrating another kind of birthday with the Lord and then concluded the service with these words, "We just want to say Happy Birthday, Tommy."

Help with Funeral Details

Another way friends might provide solace and hearten the grief-stricken is to help them with the details of the funeral. The kind of service the survivors want is their decision, and you should, of course, avoid giving unsolicited advice. You might, however, be able to give a helping hand. Tommy Hollingsworth's girlfriend, for example, told Tommy's parents that once when they heard a certain operatic aria, Tommy had said, "That's one of my father's favorites." The girlfriend told Tommy's parents that she had a recording of that aria, done in bells. They decided to play this piece at Tommy's funeral. Says Mr. Hollingsworth, "I can still hear the beautiful rendition of that song, and I can hear Tommy's voice saying, 'That's one of my father's favorites.' I'm thankful his girlfriend shared that small but significant bit of information with us."

You might also be able to help with the service in other ways. Roma's husband died after fighting a valiant battle with cancer. George and Roma both enjoyed nature and had agreed at his death to have an outdoor "celebration of life." The service was planned for a pastoral hilltop near Austin, Texas, and not far from their home. Roma wanted to use fifty-seven large blue balloons, one for each year George had lived. Transporting fifty-seven inflated balloons to the peaceful hilltop posed a problem, but a friend who realized how much this symbolism meant to Roma not only volunteered her van, she also made certain the balloons were inflated, delivered to the right spot, and distributed among the friends who were to participate in the service. Roma was visibly touched and uplifted, and her friends—especially the one who helped with the balloons—felt gratified about how they had helped Roma.

Marilyn was not so fortunate in the "help" she received with her mother's funeral. Here is an account of what happened:

> Marilyn was a member of a church whose young minister had definite but uninformed ideas about how death should be met. When her mother died, he told Marilyn that if she were a true believer she would not mourn or have an elaborate funeral. She should have the worthless body cremated at once and then have a triumphal service, with every effort to make it a testimony of the joy of true faith rather than as a time of sorrow and grief.

> Marilyn, upset and looking to her pastor for guidance, went along with his suggestions. But all the while she felt uncomfortable. She was acting in one way and feeling in another. After the service she had the nagging sense that she had been playing a game with herself. She didn't feel as if she had had a service in keeping with her feelings for her mother. She wasn't quite sure why she felt so uncomfortable about all that

had happened, but she felt that way nevertheless.[4]

Because friends are usually not as emotionally distraught by the death as close relatives, in some cases they may be better equipped than family members to provide gentle encouragement and practical help. Another example of friends helping the grief-stricken to have an especially meaningful and comforting service was demonstrated after the death of an art teacher who had reveled in sharing her creativity with friends during her life. Her husband, Walt, wanted a service that would incorporate some of her paintings, fabric hangings, and other lovely artwork. Their children—both in their twenties—were paralyzed by their grief and could not act on the heart's desire of their father. However, upon hearing about Walt's wish, several friends discussed it further with him and pitched in together to work out the logistics. The service was a tangible tribute to the beauty this woman had brought to the lives of others. The friends felt satisfying contentment in what they had been able to do, and the service genuinely gave some healing to the hurt of Walt and his two children.

In addition to helping the survivors plan a service that will be consoling, very close friends may be helpful in ensuring that the survivors do not give in to pressure (nearly always self-imposed) for a more expensive funeral than they ordinarily would want. Loved ones are frequently still in a state of shock when the services must be planned. Grief-stricken individuals in this stage tend to be somewhat irrational in their decision making. So guidance to make choices that will help heal their hurt is one of the kindest things friends can provide.

A few weeks before my sister, Janet, was killed, for example, she had bought a lovely lavender dress. She had worn it only once, for a friend's wedding shower, I think. Mother remarked how attractive Janet had looked in this dress. My mother felt, however, as a matter of principle, she should buy a new dress for Janet's burial. Several people, including one of Mother's dearest friends, coaxed her to use the lavender dress since it seemed that is what she really wanted to do and would feel most comfortable doing. This decision turned out to be the right decision: Mother commented several times how pretty Janet looked (and indeed she did). This was a wellspring of solace to my mother.

Another instance of reassuring the grief-stricken to make decisions that will lessen the pain and provide them with lasting peace of mind occurred when my grandfather died. Grandmother expressed a wish for an extremely nice vault for him. Several relatives and the morticians tried to dissuade her, explaining that an expensive vault was unnecessary. Grandmother insisted, however, and finally gave her reason. Her mother had died soon after the family homesteaded in New Mexico at the turn of the century. As a twelve-year-old girl, Martha (as my grandmother was called then) was distressed by the austerity of the coffin as well as the entire service for her mother. When she visited her mother's grave, the progressively caved-in appearance disturbed her even more. When her father died, the trappings of that funeral were also meager. Some years later the country cemetery where he was buried was abandoned. My grandmother had his casket relocated in a newer cemetery. Grandmother related how she concluded with even more certainty that upon death she wanted a nice vault for herself and Granddad. Grandmother insisted that she realized "super vaults" (her exact words) are not necessary, but as long as she could afford one, that is what she wanted. Thank goodness no one overrode her preference. When helping heal the hurt, feelings and emotions—however unreasonable or illogical—may sometimes be more important to attend to than facts and common sense. Granddad was buried in a "super vault," and that was a source of super comfort to Grandmother.

Friends can also help heal the hurt by encouraging the bereaved to make a decision about the disposition of the body that will provide lasting solace and serenity. A situation in which this suggestion was demonstrated involved Keith, an esteemed friend in his mid-forties. Keith had lived an exemplary life, and he had enjoyed every minute of it. As a staunch supporter of the University of Nebraska football team, he had frequently joked, "When I die, cremate me and sprinkle my ashes over Memorial Stadium." This time came more quickly than Keith had anticipated. He was diagnosed as having terminal cancer, and his health deteriorated quickly. As Keith's death seemed inevitable, he said seriously to his wife something like this, "After my death, my soul will be in heaven. This body will be useless, nothing but an empty shell." Keith's comment reminds me of the inscription on Joseph Jefferson's monument near Cape Cod, Massachusetts: "We are but tenants, and shortly the great Landlord will give us notice that our lease has expired."

After Keith died, some of his friends took lightly his expressed desire. But those who truly helped asked his widow what she wanted to do. She admitted that she was in a quandary. She could handle Keith's request to be cremated. But she feared what people would think about her having his ashes sprinkled over a football stadium, for that did not seem "appropriately dignified for the occasion," as she put it. Several close friends who piloted her through those difficult days and decisions after Keith's death inspired confidence in her to do what she wanted to do—not what she felt others thought she should do.

Several years have passed since Keith's death. His widow had this to say: "Well-meaning friends and relatives try to give heartbroken people advice. It is true that the shock of a death muddles one's thinking. In fact, you can hardly concentrate at all about what needs to be done. It is a temptation to let others make all the decisions. You simply do not even care. But my experience taught me a lot. Now I always refrain from telling bereaved people what they should do—or should not do."

She continues, "Also, I do not make judgmental comments. For instance, several people said unthinking things to me at Keith's service. I know now their comments came out of their own discomfort, but they said distressing things like, 'I can't believe you had Keith cremated' or 'I can't stand the thought of cremation' or 'I could never have my husband cremated.'" This widow concludes: "In contrast, I keep thoughts like that to myself and try to help the grief-stricken think through what would give them consolation."

Sharing her thoughts about disposition of the loved one's body, another widow had this to say in *The Survival Guide for Widows*:

> I wish I'd thought of some of these things before Bill died. Since his death, I have discovered that not all the people I once knew are in graveyards. Before, the only one I knew about who wasn't was the Canadian poet Pauline Johnson—her ashes are buried in Stanley Park in British Columbia. But there are some other picturesque resting places I have learned since. One friend whose home is beside an artificial lake put her husband's ashes in a thicket of trees on the other side of the lake from the house, all in view of her picture window. The Canadian actor Leslie Yeo told me that his wife Hilary Vernon's ashes are under a tree in the lovely farmyard garden of actress Pat Galloway and her husband, Dr. Bernhard Frischke. The ashes of Reverend Russell D. Horsburgh are buried in the crawl space under the exact center of the sanctuary of Zion United Church in Hamilton, Ontario. There is a plaque on the wall attesting to this fact. Now, why didn't I think of something like that?
>
> As it was, I was very traditional. I was taken

to pick a double plot in Stratford cemetery, and my husband lies on the stage-right side. I bought a large gray marble stone with his name and birth date and death date. For a little more I could have had my name and birth date put on it—a very popular custom there—all filled out but the last piece of information. I declined, saying I might drown in the South Seas and my body never be recovered, and that would be a terrible waste of stone cutting. I honestly don't like that empty space waiting for me.[5]

In her usual humorous way, this same widow discusses another concern which might have been averted if friends had helped her explore another means for the disposition of her dead husband's body:

> The real cruncher is that I'm a terrible gardener. Every time I go and look at the sad geraniums I put in each year and the struggling Japanese yews I planted, I say to my husband: "Well, you always knew what a terrible gardener I am."[6]

Be With Those Who Can't Attend

Another way friends may help is by staying with an individual who is not able to attend a loved one's funeral. A dear relative, for example, had a troublesome pregnancy. A premature and difficult delivery resulted in a weakened baby who lived only a few short hours. My relative was still bedfast the day of the funeral for little Tammy. Two very wise friends came to stay with the sorrowful mother during the time the services were taking place. "Their being with me during that desolate hour is still heartwarming to me," says my relative, now a mother of three grown daughters and grandmother to several healthy grandchildren.

A similar case involved a couple who had been in a car wreck. The husband was killed, whereas the wife was in intensive care for several days. Even though her condition was critical, she was aware of her husband's death and insisted on going to the service—which, of course, was out of the question. To console her, several friends stayed by her bedside during the time of the service. One of the friends knew the order of service, so the friends held a "mini-service" right in the hospital room. They talked about some of the outstanding contributions of the husband's life, read the same Scriptures that were being recited at his funeral, played some of Lee's favorite songs, and they prayed. "While most people felt they should attend Lee's funeral," says the widow, "I was thankful for the friends who went to the trouble to get the information to hold a beautiful service right there in my hospital room." She adds, "I needed compassionate friends close to me during that hour more than at any other time of my life. I am certain that thoughtful gesture helped me on the road to recovery."

Go With the Bereaved to View the Body

Sometimes it's helpful to accompany the bereaved when they go to view the body for the first time. A couple offered to go with Joan and her husband to view the body of Joan's mother. Joan lived in the same town as her mother, and she was with her in the hospital when she died. Several close friends gathered at Frank and Joan's home later that evening. During the conversations about the death and the funeral arrangements Sharon overheard Joan say something like this: "I dread going to see Mother lying in that casket."

Sharon's first husband had died, and she recalls resisting going to see his body. He was young and in the prime of life when he was killed in a hunting accident. "I wanted to remember my husband as he was," she claimed. Sharon later admitted that she was thankful others encouraged her to view his body. Sharon knew from experience the pain of seeing a loved one dead, but she also understood the importance of viewing the body. She remembers thinking about her deceased husband, "I could not realize he was really dead until I saw him lying there in the casket." One grief counselor explains the value of viewing the body:

> The moment of truth that comes when the living persons face the dead body can be one of the most significant and therapeutically useful parts of the process of coping with death. Until the whole person is willing to face the facts of the change that death brings, it is difficult or impossible to begin the true work of mourning. A simple way of expressing it is to say you must go through the emotional equivalent of a Good Friday to be able to have the resurrection experience of an Easter.[7]

Before Sharon and her husband left Frank and Joan's home that evening, Sharon offered, "Would you like for us to go with you to the funeral home tomorrow?" Joan and her husband readily accepted and were grateful for the presence of empathic friends during that difficult but essential hurdle.

Be Sensitive to Delayed Grief

Friends with similar, keen perception also helped a grief-stricken person in another situation. A friend of mine told about a friend of his who flew to Alaska for a twelve-month assignment. Just off the coast his plane crashed; his body was never recovered. A memorial service was held in Austin. Here's how the widow remembers her reaction: "During the service especially and for weeks afterwards, I was in a state of disbelief. . . . it all seemed so unreal. Perhaps it was 'magical thinking,' but the thought kept running through my mind, 'This is one big mistake . . . he'll come back home in twelve months, just as we always planned.'" The widow continues, "When my husband did not return after twelve months—when I had originally anticipated his return—the reality of his death hit me like a bombshell. I no longer could deny his death. I finally had to face the horrible fact that he would never come home."

My friend and some other sensitive friends became aware of her intense grief. They invited her to join them for the weekend at their lake home. There they encouraged her to talk about whatever she needed to. She talked about the early years of their marriage, about their two children, about her husband's death, about her future without him. "When the memorial service was held," said the widow, "many friends came to it. I appreciated them all. Little did I know I would also need them in my despair twelve months later." She concluded, "I was lucky to have some very insightful and compassionate friends."

When the Funeral Is Out of Town

Leon, a Seattle businessman, told of some very practical ways friends helped him when his father died. "My father lived in Rhode Island," explains Leon, "so my Seattle friends could not very well attend his funeral." Continues Leon, "But they did a lot of things to get me on my way!" He elaborated how one friend took the suit he wanted to wear to his father's service to the cleaners, requested a rush job, and then picked it up and brought it to Leon's house. "While he was waiting for the suit to be cleaned, he took my shoes to be shined. I never would've thought about the shoes, but he knew how much I like nice-looking shoes."

Another friend arranged for Leon's mail to be kept at the post office until his return. Leon's next-door neighbor offered to get his newspapers off his lawn every morning while he was gone. Another friend spent nearly an hour on the phone, making travel arrangements for Leon. "I was so stunned by my father's death that thinking straight enough to choose airplane flights would've been almost more than I could handle."

Another friend and his wife drove Leon to the airport and took his dog to the kennel. "This same couple met me at the airport when I returned," continues Leon, "and not only had they washed and cleaned up my car, they had picked up my dog." Adds Leon, "None of these friends even knew my father, but they took hold of the myriad 'loose ends' and helped me cope with his death. They made me realize that ministering to a grief-stricken person doesn't require eloquent words or dramatic gestures of sympathy. And sometimes attending the service is not possible. In my case, what I needed was someone to get my suit cleaned, my shoes shined, and to take care of my dog."

During the Funeral

Housesitting is another helpful act related to the funeral. Right before I completed my master's degree from Mills College, in Oakland, California, a classmate's grandfather died, and several of us planned to attend the funeral. The boyfriend of one of the girls had just graduated from a police academy. He and two of his friends and also his seventeen-year-old brother housesat during the funeral. The grandparents' home was in Piedmont, a nice area and a prime target of home robberies during funerals. My friend's grandmother was truly appreciative of this considerate deed.

Caring for young children of the grief-stricken during the funeral may also be something friends or relatives can do to ease the burden. My mother, for example, says she was still in a state of shock at my father's funeral, but she was aware of several relatives who gave me special attention. Says my mother, "Knowing that someone was taking care of you provided welcomed relief and is one of the few things I can remember being grateful for that day."

Whether or not you take children to a funeral depends on several considerations—the age of the child, the ability of the child to comprehend what the funeral is all about, the relationship of the child to the deceased, and whether or not there is a calm, reassuring person to accompany the child throughout the service. These are but a few of the considerations to keep in mind. Experts say that funerals hold little meaning for children under four and that the heightened emotions may be upsetting to them. On the other hand, experts also contend that children are more apt to feel fearful and frustrated if left out than by including them.

Talking to the child, explaining what will be taking place, and then letting him or her decide whether or not to attend the service may be a good approach. One of my brothers provides a good example of this. His wife was killed in an automobile accident. Their five children ranged in age from three to twelve years old at the time. My brother, Bill, made the decision that the three-year-old would not attend his mother's funeral, but he talked to the other older children and let them make the choice for themselves. As adults now they all agree their father handled the situation the best way.

In contrast, one mother who made the decision that her son and daughter would not view their dead brother's body has this to say:

In the healing years since Robby died, I have

reviewed what we did correctly and, as well, the areas in which we erred. Because of my protective instinct as a mother, I made a massive error in judgment. I would not allow my son, aged twelve, to view the body of his dead brother because of the horror I felt seeing it. Difficult though it would have been, he should not have been denied this right. Unfortunately, no one told me I would harm my son with my protectiveness. And harm him it did because it took many years for him to lay his brother's ghost to rest.

My daughter, then four, did not attend the funeral and therefore had even less grasp of her brother's death. She is resentful even after all these years that she was cheated of the experience.[8]

Another child gives this account of her father's death:

My father died about a year ago. . . . I was nine and a half at the time. My brother and I were away visiting my uncle . . . and my mom called up and said we had to come home. She didn't tell us why or anything, and when we got home she told us the bad news. My father had actually died a week before we got home, but Mom didn't call us right away. She didn't want us to have to go to the funeral because she thought it would make it worse for us. I don't even know where my dad's buried, which upsets me. It would be nice to see where he is.[9]

When I was in the fourth grade, one of my classmates died. He had a ruptured appendix. Harold was his name. One day Harold was at school, playing, talking, and teasing the girls. Two days later the teacher told us, "Harold is dead." I can still vividly remember my disbelief: "This just can't be true." At the recess after hearing the bad news we shared our thoughts. One boy was certain Harold had run away. Other comments reflected similar disbelief and fantasies of Harold's merely hiding somewhere. "He can't be dead," I remember saying confidently. The moment of truth came, though, when some of us attended the funeral. We could no longer deny the reality of Harold's death when we saw his still, lifeless body.

Years later when I was an adult, the fiancé of the daughter of one of my friends was reported missing in Afghanistan. Her thoughts were much like mine when the teacher told us about Harold. "He can't be dead," she said to her mother. For six months grief and despair were interspersed with hope. Even when word came that positive identification had been made of Ryan's body, she still harbored a glint of hope. "Maybe they made a mistake," she thought. When Ryan's parents received his belongings and his military tags, her ray of hope dimmed—but it did not go out. "When I see his body, then I will admit that he is dead," she said. People of all ages, including children, are more convinced of the death if they see the body and attend the funeral. This gives them some closure and frees them to move forward in their grieving.

Prayers

The expression of prayer is nearly always a vital part of any service for a dead person. Carefully-worded and sincerely-spoken prayers help console and encourage the grief-stricken. One relative of Ashley (the teenager we discussed earlier who committed suicide) recalls how the prayer invoked at the graveside services for all to hear helped her immensely. The requests went something like this: "Dear God, our

Heavenly Father, please forgive us, and help us to forgive ourselves for ways we may have failed Ashley. Help sanctify our memories of Ashley. Because of her death, help us to face the future not with despair but with renewed zeal to live life fully and compassionately as Ashley did."

Another bereaved person also says that the prayers expressed at the service of her loved one offered solace, and the fact that others were gathered together and heard the prayers bolstered her faith and courage. "Especially during the prayers," said Marti, "I felt enfolded by the love of all the people at my mother's funeral." Another relative attending the funeral said that she felt God's presence more during the prayers than at any other time in the service. Her comments were a powerful reminder of the promise offered in Matthew 18:20, "For where two or three are gathered together in my name, there am I in the midst of them."

One word of caution about prayer. The funeral may not be the time or place to suggest personally to the grief-stricken to pray for comfort. This early in their grief the loved ones may still be in shock. They may already have been praying for months for God's healing— now they may be struggling with why God let this death happen. Their well of faith may be dry. So, depending on the circumstances, telling grief-stricken persons you will be praying for them may be the most encouraging comment you can make. One of my favorite pastors in years gone by put it this way: "Talking to people for God is a great thing, but talking to God for people is greater still."

For example, one mother whose thirteen-year-old daughter died, says, "I simply could not pray for days. At first I was angry with God. Then I simply had no feeling. My faith was flat." She adds, "But I welcomed with open heart all the offers of others to pray for me." She goes on to explain how many of the same people who told her at the funeral that they would pray for her formed a prayer chain. When the distraught mother would dip into pits of despair, she had only to call any one of the members to set a twenty-four-hour prayer chain into action. "The prayers at my daughter's funeral," she says, "set the tone for later prayers. Oh, how I needed them. I could literally feel the power of prayer uplifting me."

The experience of this mother and that of many others reinforces the truth reflected in Alfred Tennyson's oft-quoted words: "More things are wrought by prayer than this world dreams of." Moreover, James, the brother of Jesus, said: "Earnest prayer has great power and wonderful results." (James 5:16, *The Living Bible*)

Expressions of Gratitude and Grief

Funerals can also be healing, says Pastor Mike Toby, because they provide an opportunity for a spokesperson for the family, usually the officiating clergy, to tell the friends thank you for all their gestures of sympathy, including their attendance at the service. The bereaved may not be able to express their appreciation to everyone who has helped in some way or to all those who attend the service. Voicing this gratitude publicly for all to hear, says Pastor Toby, is healing to the surviving loved ones.

Friends who truly want to help the grief-stricken will allow them to express their grief at the funeral in ways meaningful to them. Sometimes these ways can be simple or small. Remember the old saying, "It's not the great storm that destroys the giant oak tree—it's the little bugs." A once popular song put it a more positive way: "Little things mean a lot." Martha Lou Scott's mother, for example, wanted to leave her husband's wedding band on for his burial. Some of her friends insisted, "But everyone always takes off the wedding rings to keep." Martha Lou's mother left her husband's ring on and defended her decision like this: "He has not had his wedding ring off for over thirty years, and I wouldn't feel right taking it off now."

Martha Lou also remembers how her mother always straightened her father's tie right before he would leave the house for his day's work—partly because the tie needed a little adjusting but mostly as a gesture of love and approval and a wish for a good day. Before the casket was closed, Martha Lou's mother straightened her beloved husband's tie. That was something she simply had to do as part of their longstanding ritual, and she was thankful no one discouraged her but understood the importance of it.

Children especially should also be permitted to grieve in ways meaningful to them. I remember someone telling the story about a teenager who could not be found when it was time to attend the funeral for a buddy who had committed suicide. A friend finally found him on a bridge, throwing dollar bills down on the flowing water below. He mumbled something like, "Nothing else matters now." The friend wisely did not act shocked, nor did he reprimand the boy but tried to see things from his viewpoint. The friend said something like, "It's tough losing a friend, isn't it? Especially like this."

Another child wanted—and needed—to write a note to his mother after she died. Here is an account of how the father helped the child:

> The night before the funeral we all went to the funeral parlor and I spent a lot of time right next to her coffin. She was wearing a white dress, but that's about all I remember. I remember her more when she was alive because I think my mind wants to remember her alive rather than dead. I'm glad, though, that I got a chance to get a last look at her. I drew a picture for her and wrote a little note on it asking her to wait in heaven for all of us. I gave it to Daddy to put in the coffin with her, and even though she was dead, I like

to think that she got that last message from me.[10]

Recognizing grief as a normal reaction to loss and allowing individuals to express their feelings at the services and in the following days and weeks is vital to grief recovery. Friends sometimes think once the funeral is over then the grief-stricken are "on the road to recovery." Not so. Grief recovery often takes much longer than friends realize. Here's how one person continued to handle her grief:

> My mother died when I was a teenager. Dad has done a wonderful job with my brothers and me, but I miss my mom. I hate it that she isn't here for special times like graduation and my engagement. So I visit the cemetery often to "talk" with her. I straighten up the grave site and then sit and tell her about my life, my troubles, and my joys. Sometimes I cry; sometimes I laugh. Without fail, I leave feeling better.
>
> Some people would think I'm crazy, I suppose. But my mother is still alive in my heart, and she's still an important part of my life—always will be.[11]

Music

Music helps people express their emotions by giving release to emotions difficult to put into words. This may be especially true at funerals, for listening to the music as they are surrounded by friends and relatives who care about them helps people in a variety of ways. The family of the deceased usually chooses music with a specific reason in mind. For example, they may want a joyous, victorious song or one that is a praise song. Or the family may select a certain song because it reminds them of the deceased, or it was a favorite song of the loved one.

For instance, Ralph, well-known and well-liked music minister in Texas and throughout the Southwest, selected "Going Home" to sing at his mother's funeral. Years before, Ralph had sung this beautiful song at his senior recital at seminary, and his mother's comment then was, "That's one of my favorites. I want it sung at my funeral." Ralph remembered his mother's wish and sang it as a tribute to her and to her Christian beliefs. "Sharing this song for all to hear the beauty and the message in it, particularly in the refrain, 'I'm just going home,' was consoling to all of us who loved my mother," explained Ralph. He elaborated, "For five years before her death, Mother suffered from Alzheimer's disease, so this song was especially comforting. Sharing through song the thought at her funeral that she indeed was 'going home' gave me peace."

Courage to Face the Future

Music also helps create an atmosphere of worship. In other words, the words and the melody remind all those attending the service that "God is great and God is good," and as one song says, "God will take care of you." Some people need that reassurance merely to attend a funeral. Few people like to go to funerals, but I know some who simply refuse to attend funerals. They may feel awkward and fear they will do or say the wrong thing. Or they may fear losing control and crying excessively. This dread may be caused by unresolved grief from other deaths in days gone by. Or some people may be gripped with the thought that death could claim their husband, or child, or parent. For instance, a friend once told me she simply could not attend the service for the daughter of a mutual friend. "It would remind me too painfully that my daughter could also die," she said.

People who will not attend services for relatives or close friends perhaps need to examine their attitudes and try to figure out why. As

Socrates advised us, "Know thyself." I used to find all kinds of "good" reasons not to attend funerals, and then because of deaths in my own family I became more aware of how much attendance means to the bereaved.

Now I also see an additional benefit of attending funerals: They remind me to live life fully now, for someday I too shall die! Job expressed it this way: "Man, who is born of woman, is short-lived. Like a flower he comes forth and withers. His days are determined, and his limits Thou has set." (Job 14:1, 2, 5, *New American Standard Bible*) The writer of Chronicles said it like this: "For we are here for but a moment, strangers in the land as our fathers were before us; our days on earth are like a shadow, gone so soon." (First Chronicles 29:15, *The Living Bible*)

So, funerals can be powerful reminders to us to live our lives so that we can face death with no regrets of how we have lived our lives. Commenting on this idea, Abraham Maslow, the great psychologist, said: "The confrontation with death makes everything look so precious, so sacred, so beautiful that I feel more strongly than ever to love life, to embrace it and to let myself be overwhelmed by it."

Some years ago my husband's uncle died. Uncle Dick truly "knew life" and embraced it. He had lived eighty-three full years, enjoying most every minute as he taught university classes, worked in his community, served his church, and helped and encouraged others, including my husband and me. The services held for him in San Diego, California, were a fitting tribute to him as numerous individuals shared a few sentences about how he had touched their lives. One person, for instance, told how Uncle Dick always brought the best out in people and that he had never heard Uncle Dick criticize anyone. Others mentioned similar attributes, and some shared how Uncle Dick's sense of humor had seen them through difficult situations. One person shared the wording of a plaque that hung in Uncle Dick's study. These words reflect Uncle Dick's wit but also his sincere desire to please God:

I pray that I may live to fish
Until my dying day.
And when it comes to my last cast,
I then most humbly pray,
When in the Lord's great landing net
And peacefully asleep,
That in His mercy I be judged,
Big enough to keep!

We do indeed need to make our own peace with death, life, and God for our own good, but also to be able to give comfort and encouragement to others in their dark hours of grief. As this chapter emphasizes, one of the most powerful ways to do that is to go to the funeral—or at least make it easier for grief-stricken friends to go.

One of my sisters, Brenda, said, "The presence of friends and relatives at Janet and Robert's services told me that I had friends—and relatives—I could count on. Each one was a tangible reminder that life itself is a gift of God, and life must go on." Brenda continued, "Their caring enough to be there with me and my family was heart-touching and affirmed my belief that whatever happens, God is in control."

Brenda's experience is similar to that of countless others who recognize the value of friends and relatives attending services. Their presence gives inexpressible comfort to the bereaved and courage to face the future without their loved one.

Step 4
❧

Give a Hug
The healing touch...

I never knew my father since I was eight months old when he was killed. As I grew older, I asked my mother lots of questions, including what helped her handle the heart-piercing grief caused by his sudden and tragic death. "I don't remember anything that was said," my mother recalled of those awful days and weeks after he died. "What I do remember are the heartfelt hugs. They helped me more than anything else."

Others have also recognized the caring and healing power of touch, reflecting its importance in a variety of ways. Remember the bumper sticker popular a few years ago: "Have you hugged your kid today?" In addition, there is that old familiar saying many of us grew up with: "Actions speak louder than words." Extolling beautifully the magic of touch, Luciano de Crescenzo said, "We are each of us angels with only one wing. And we can only fly embracing each other."

Similarly, our everyday language reveals an instinctive

awareness of the power of touch to convey deep meaning. Consider the expressions "keeping in touch," a "touching experience," and "being touched." Even advertisements have capitalized on this compelling human need—for instance, the once ubiquitous telephone slogan, "Reach out and touch someone."

Nowhere is the force of touch demonstrated more powerfully than in the Bible. Nearly every time Jesus healed someone, for example, touch was involved. He "stretched out his hand and touched" the leper, (Matthew 8:3, *Revised Standard Version*) and when Peter's mother-in-law was sick, Jesus "touched her hand, and the fever left her." (Matthew 8:15, *Revised Standard Version*) In addition, when mothers brought their children to Jesus, "He took them in His arms and blessed them, laying His hands upon them." (Mark 10:16, *Revised Standard Version*)

A well-timed embrace, a pat on the back, a handclasp, a playful poke in the stomach, or a hand on the shoulder as you talk can be more valuable to a suffering person than silver or gold, or any other gift. The lame man described in Acts, for example, expected a gift from Peter and John: "But Peter said, 'I have no silver and gold, but I give you what I have. . . .' And he took him by the right hand and raised him up." (Acts 3:6–7, *Revised Standard Version*)

"Wait a minute," you may be saying right about now, "I am just not a 'touchy-feely' person." It is true, we Americans tend to touch less than most other cultures. Many families are characterized by a *Noli mi tangere*, a "Do not touch me" way of life. In contrast, embraces and other gestures of touch are a part of everyday interaction in many countries. Sadly enough, Americans tend to think of bodily contact in terms of sex or combat—and both are prickly with psychological and cultural taboos. Experts on grieving tell us, however, that touch, if used appropriately and sensitively, can provide healing of hurts just as it did in days long past.

Emphasis is on sensitivity, for physical gushing can be even more offensive than verbal gushing. A truth stated long ago is just as applicable now as it was then:

> "To everything there is a season, and a time to every purpose under the heaven . . . a time to embrace, and a time to refrain from embracing." (Ecclesiastes 3:1, 5)

Comfort Without Words

Norman Vincent Peale shared with me how touch was a consolation and an encouragement to him when his mother died. "I had visited my mother Friday evening in upstate New York, in the little town of Canisteo," Dr. Peale began, "and then I had taken a train back to New York City. When I got to our apartment on Fifth Avenue, my wife telephoned me to the relay the news—my mother had died early Saturday morning. I went to my office at the church, and I picked up a copy of the Bible my mother had given me years before." As Dr. Peale sat there, reflecting on his mother's death, a strong sense of peace came over him. "I felt two cupped hands on my head. They were unmistakably my mother's hands . . . to comfort me," said Dr. Peale. Then this great man, whose books and teachings have for decades given meaning and power to the lives of literally thousands, said simply, "It can be argued as fantasy, but it was neither fantasy nor imagined."

Dr. Peale said he decided at that moment his mother would want him to keep his speaking engagement in Elberon, a town some distance away. He elaborated, "My mother had taught me to keep commitments when people were counting on me." While waiting in Penn Station, Dr. Peale met a long-time friend, Colonel Myron Robinson, and he asked, "Where are you going?" His friend answered, and then asked Dr. Peale the same question. Come to find out, they had different destinations, but they would be taking the same train.

After they boarded, Colonel Robinson commented to Dr. Peale, "You are not your usual self." At this observation, Dr. Peale told his friend about his mother's death. Dr. Peale noted that his friend said nothing, but simply laid his hand on Dr. Peale's knee. The two rode on in emotion-packed silence. "When I got off the train," said Dr. Peale, "so did Colonel Robinson. I questioned him, 'I thought you were going somewhere else?' Colonel Robinson responded, 'I'd rather hear you speak.'"

Dr. Peale told me his friend stayed with him through the speech and the lunch. When it was time to go, Colonel Robinson said something like this to Dr. Peale, "Son, you've helped me through some tough ones, and I know you are going through a difficult time."

"With those words," said Dr. Peale, "my friend hit me lightly in the chest." Then Dr. Peale concluded his thoughts on the importance of touch in his time of grief by saying, "Those gentle loving hands of my mother and those strong, manly gestures from a big, tough friend showed me clearly the comfort and strength that can come from touch."[1]

Profound messages of care and concern were conveyed clearly to Dr. Peale—with very few words! In similar situations most of us feel compelled to utter some pious platitudes like, "It was for the best," or "She'd lived a full life," or "At least she went quickly," or "She's in heaven now." Furthermore, we sometimes fall into an even deeper pit by offering verbose explanations why the death had to happen, or by struggling to outline a formula, shortcutting grief recovery. In other words, we try to provide an easy path to bypass grief—where there is no detour. Colonel Robinson did none of these, and Dr. Peale remembers him as one who gave the utmost comfort. This dear friend followed the wise example of Walt Whitman: "I do not give lectures. When I give, I give myself."[2] In the words of Oscar Wilde, "He knew the precise psychological moment when to say nothing."[3]

Touch Frees Bereaved to Talk

Not only does touch sometimes keep us from talking too much, it may help the bereaved to feel freer to talk. Grieving persons may need desperately to talk out their heart-searing emotions after the death of a loved one. This was especially true in the case of Merle Whitman, a New Mexico rancher.

Merle asked J.D., his neighbor, to help load his horse in a trailer. The horse "spooked," as they say, and turned around and around, knocking J.D. against the fence. When this happened, J.D. slumped over in a limp heap. Merle ran to the house to telephone for help. J.D. was pronounced dead of a heart attack soon after the ambulance arrived at the hospital.

Merle played J.D.'s death scene over and over again in his mind. Having had opportunities to learn CPR, Merle had never taken advantage of them. An engulfing sense of responsibility haunted him day and night. "If I had known CPR, J.D. would be alive today," said Merle. He hated himself for J.D.'s death, for the grief J.D.'s widow was experiencing, and for the financial bind J.D.'s family now faced. Merle even hated the horse.

"But what I detested most," adds Merle, "is how everyone kept telling me not to blame myself." Merle goes on to describe the one person—a neighbor named Will—who offered him the most relief. This weathered old rancher with little formal education but vast wisdom kept coming by to see Merle. Sitting at the kitchen table with cups of steaming hot coffee, Will and Merle often talked together. "I remember so well," recalls Merle, "how Will listened patiently, never interrupting with 'You don't need to feel that way.' Then my friend would get up to leave, rinse out his coffee cup, put on his hat, come to me and without a word put his hand on my shoulder, grasping it firmly and giving it a little tug back and forth." Merle concluded: "I knew by Will's gesture that he cared about me and he understood what I was going through—that firm grip and gentle shake encouraged me more than I can explain to you."

Psychological Studies

Touch indeed helps in a mysterious but profound way. Harry F. Harlow, an American psychologist, studied the deep human yearning for touch. All psychologists and students who have had a psychology course or two know about him and his famous research. This psychologist built two surrogate or substitute mothers for baby monkeys. One, a mother figure built of wire, gave milk, while the other, built of sponge rubber and terry cloth, gave no milk. Given a choice, the baby monkeys went to the terry cloth mother for the comfort of her soft "touch," preferring touch to food. Generalizing his findings from animal studies to humans, Dr. Harlow contradicted the accepted theory that a baby loves its mother because she provides food. He concluded that contact comfort was a more important part of this love, and that nursing was, perhaps, less important as a source of food than as a source of reassuring touch.[4]

I neither want to oversimplify nor overgeneralize from this famous research, but it does suggest that along with the food we take to bereaved people we need to provide a hug or two—and that the hug might meet a need more urgent than the need for food. In fact, the grief-stricken may not have an appetite for food, but they usually never refuse a hug.

Medical Research

Medical doctors as well as other health professionals are

who say, "I'm just not a hugger or a toucher," shut themselves off from opportunities that might prove rewarding for themselves as well as their bereaved friends.

As we continue to expand our storehouse of perceptive human responses, we may discover more and more about ourselves and how touch, when used appropriately, transcends many human facades— offering comfort, support, sympathy, and a whole rainbow of other human encouragement. At the risk of sounding glib, I offer the oft-repeated advertising slogan and endorse its heartfelt and appropriate application to touch: "Try it, you'll like it."

One widow complained on how she would have liked more hugs from caring people:

> Your mind is still on crutches. . . . There is something awe-inspiring, silencing, and shattering about emotional pain that does leave one a loss for words. Perhaps gestures are better. I've mentioned before my need for hugs. I'm sure other people feel the same way. Human physical comfort, no strings. I saw a cartoon once, no caption. . . . It was a vending machine; the sign on it read: "Hugs 25 cents." I wish I could have one installed.[9]

When Words Add Anguish

A hug or other forms of touch can be very handy when words might add awkwardness or even anguish to the situation. A friend told me about a painful incident in her life when an understanding hand on her shoulder helped tremendously. "After our first baby was stillborn, I had to force myself out of my malaise and back to work," Jill began. "At coffee break my first morning back some of the girls were talking about their being pregnant. I thought they were insensitive to just keep on talking about their pregnancies." Jill continued, "When I thought I couldn't stand it any longer, Paula, the person sitting next to me, put her hand on my shoulder in a warm, compassionate way." Jill elaborated, "If Paula had said something to make them stop talking about their pregnancies, I would've been embarrassed, and it would've been even worse." Concluded Jill, "That friendly, all-knowing hand on my shoulder steadied my nerves and kept me from falling apart. Paula became an even dearer friend after that."

The touch of a reassuring hand also steadied Anita and helped her through a difficult moment. Six months after Anita's teenage daughter, Gayle, had died suddenly, Anita was sitting in church on Mother's Day. It was the first Mother's Day since Gayle's death, but Anita felt in control—that is, until a group of four-year-olds sang "Jesus Loves Me." As had happened numerous times before, Anita's grief was triggered all anew. She remembered vividly how Gayle as a four-year-old had sung that same song with a group of other children. However, Gayle had also sung a solo, and Anita and her husband had recorded it. They had listened to the recording just a few weeks before in the privacy of their family room. "We cried our eyes out," comments Anita. But when she found herself in church, listening to that same song and a new supply of tears began to push hard against the floodgate, there was no way to escape—people were sitting all around her. Anita continues, "A friend sitting next to me felt me trembling. She looked at me out of the corner of her eyes until our eyes locked. I knew she understood my agony." A line from Tennyson's "In Memoriam" seems to be written for that moment: "Her eyes are homes of silent prayer." Adds Anita, "Then the friend put her hand over mine—and the heartache and the wall of tears subsided."

Breaking Communication Barriers

A kind touch, a hug, or an appropriate handclasp can also break communication barriers. Ken and Martha, for example, noticed sitting behind them at church a person they had never seen before. After the service, Ken turned to him, saying, "I don't believe I've met you." Ken recalled later that the man looked panicky. Ken instinctively reached out his hand. "The man gripped my hand," says Ken, "like he was holding on for dear life. And he kept clutching it as we talked." Ken and Martha were going out to eat after church, so they invited the man to accompany them. As this story unfolded, Rod, as the man was called, shared how he and his teenage son, Ryan, had moved to the area two years ago. He and his wife had divorced the year before that. Only months after the move, the son was diagnosed as having leukemia. After an up-and-down battle, the son died. "I felt like my entire world had caved in," the distraught man admitted. "I came to church just to be with people—that house is unbearably empty since Ryan died."

Ken and Martha befriended Rod, introduced him to some of their friends, and they finally even became relatives. Ken's sister, Kathy, had been married only a short time when her husband was killed in military combat. Kathy had never remarried. When she and Rod met, they seemed a perfect match. In fact, they had been happily married seven years when she shared this whole story with me. She told how grateful Rod was that Sunday when Ken reached out his hand to him: "Rod said that outstretched hand was a turning point—it gave him hope and renewed his faith that somebody cared for him." Not in all cases, of course, does an extended hand create such a beautiful story, but we never know when it just might.

Easing the Hurt of Emptiness

Although the response to an outstretched hand is not always predictable, one thing nearly always is for certain after a death. That is a feeling of emptiness—or aloneness, or a feeling of being severed from all that matters. "If all the cataclysmic emotions of grief that leave even the strongest psyche tattered had to be described in one word, that one word might be emptiness," said one person. Grief-stricken individuals, of course, are not the only ones who suffer from haunting feelings of emptiness, but a death nearly always precipitates acute and persistent bouts of these feelings. In fact, the word widow, I have heard, comes from the Sanskrit and means "empty." I also read somewhere that the word widow comes from the Latin *viduus*, again meaning "empty."

Whatever its roots, the word widow conjures up images of a wide range of these feelings—especially to those who have experienced them. Consider how one widow described her feelings of "emptiness":

> After my husband died, I felt like one of those
> spiraled shells washed up on the beach. Poke a straw
> through the twisting tunnel, around and around, and
> there is nothing there. No flesh. No life. Whatever
> lived there is dried up and gone.[10]

Nearly two thousand women become widows every day in the United States. Moreover, there are more than twelve million widows in all and about two and one-half million widowers. In addition, thousands of people have lost other loved ones—children, parents, brothers, sisters, grandparents, best friends. Most of these grief-stricken individuals know all too well the pain of emptiness— the stillness of the loved one's car, the silence at the back door, the empty place at the dining table, the unoccupied chair in front of the television, the vacant place in the car, the unrumpled bed.

Friends who want to alleviate some of the anguish of that black void of emptiness may see obvious ways to do just that. Annie Ruth Ruff, a widow, says, for example, that when she met Dennis Myers in the hall at church, he frequently said something like, "You look like you need a hug." Then he promptly met that need. Annie Ruth emphasized, "Dennis was always right—I did need a hug, and his giving me one always helps!"

Sometimes small, practical ways to lessen feelings of emptiness produce large results. I remember the sadness in Grandmother's eyes when right after Granddad died, she would look at his empty chair in the living room. A brilliant (but very common sense) insight came to me: "Why don't we rearrange the furniture, Grandmother?" Calling on some others, we all, shoulder-to-shoulder, arranged the living room furniture in a new way. Grandmother's comment was simply, "This helps."

Later the same day, I noticed another seemingly small gesture offering great comfort to Grandmother. A visiting friend was sitting by Grandmother on the sofa. She had gently put her hand on Grandmother's hand as we reminisced.

At another time during those first few days after Granddad died, several of us went into the kitchen to gather around the table for coffee—a longstanding ritual in Grandmother and Granddad's house. As we all started picking out our chairs, a tense awkwardness started building up. Granddad had always sat at a certain place at the table, and, of course, that place was now empty. None of us wanted that place left empty—but neither did anyone want to appear presumptuous and sit in it. Finally a quick-thinking in-law broke the stony silence, saying to my husband, "Del, I think Granddad wouldn't care if you sat in his place." Standing close to Grandmother, Del put his arm around her, asking, "What do you think, Grandmother?" With the first twinkle in her eyes and smile on her lips since Granddad's death, Grandmother motioned approval for Del to sit in Granddad's place.

In yet another example, hugs helped dissipate some of the Hollingsworth's grief and loneliness after their only son, Tommy, was murdered. (The Step 3 chapter spells out their story more completely.) When the Hollingsworths returned to the mission field in Argentina after Tommy's death, parents there seemed to usher their children out of sight. Finally, Mrs. Hollingsworth told the well-intentioned parents, "We love your children, and we need their closeness and their hugs." Instead of being painful reminders of their own son's death, the children helped fill the awful emptiness, say the Hollingsworths.

A Soothing Balm for Children

Embraces, hugs, or hands held may, in turn, also help children cope with death. Touch, in fact, may be one of the most effective ways to help young children handle their emotions. Some people say, "But they are too young to understand death." To that I would reply, "Do any of us—at any age—really understand death?" In addition, I would emphasize, "Children are never too young to feel."

All of us who have been around young children know they are extremely sensitive to the emotional climate. Children can sense any marked variation in the mood and attitudes of those around them. Undergoing any change or loss usually threatens their sense of security, and they, in turn, may react in ways that are confusing to us or in ways we feel are wholly inappropriate for the situation. However, just like adults who may be irascible after the death of someone close, children who are irritable need an extra dose of warm, affectionate concern and caring. An incident from my own childhood illustrates this. I cannot remember all the details, but I do vividly recall my feelings.

Our first-grade class was having a party, and the day before the party one of the mothers organizing it insisted, "Now be sure to invite your father and mother." I remember feeling downcast; I concluded that I was about the only one in the whole world who did not have both a mother and a father, and then the day of the party it seemed that everybody else's mother and father were there. I probably was not acting as I should've been, and that same well-meaning mother commented something like this to me, "Well, at least you could try to have a good time. We've worked hard on this party." Thank goodness, I had the most marvelous teacher—Miss Alta Glascow—I shall never forget her name, her kind smile, or her ingenious understanding of children. In a way so typical of how I remember her, she came over to me, put her warm, caring arm around me and just stood there for a moment. Then, reinforcing that reassuring gesture, she said something beautiful like, "Would you come over here? I need someone special to help me."

Another personal instance I can recall also illustrates how touch can add soothing balm to the wounded sensitivity of children. Unthinking adults would describe in front of me the fiery collision that claimed the life of my twenty-seven-year-old father. The setting was always about the same. People would gather around in small groups at a social or family get-together. Usually children would be all over the place. Adults would identify each child. The typical identifying remark about me was, "Oh, that's Barbara . . . Johnny's girl, you know, he was the one killed on the Floyd highway." Then an explicit description of the wreck would follow by one or more adults oblivious to my presence or feelings.

After one of these episodes, one adult did recognize that I was upset. My mother, one of the kindest, most compassionate persons I have ever known, overheard this conversation. Drawing away from the few people she was talking to, she slipped inconspicuously to my side, clasped her hand around mine and led me out of the room. Hand in hand, we zigzagged our way around the cars parked helter-skelter in front of my grandparents' country home and headed down a well-worn road. No words were spoken. No words were needed. My mother's hand around mine said it all.

Jayton was seven when his dad died. His brother was nine. "The most comforting thing to me," comments Jayton, many years later, "was how my mother let me stay close to her. Everything was terrifying—mother crying, people coming and going. But I hung onto her as though death might snatch her away too." Jayton adds, "What I didn't like were all these people I didn't know crying and hugging me, nearly squeezing the breath out of me. Both my brother and I were frightened, but I was the one who wanted to stay right with Mom. My brother was older and felt like he had to act big. In fact, several made comments to him like, 'Now you are the man of the house.' People meant well, but that was an awful burden to put on a skinny, scared nine-year-old boy!"

Jayton went on to say, "That first night after Dad died we all stayed with our grandparents—Mom's parents. When we finally could go to bed—people just stayed and stayed—my brother and I started out on the couch in the family room. But when we heard Mom crying, we went to her bedroom. Then we all hugged and cried until we couldn't cry any more." Adds Jayton, "Then we all just lay in the dark, talking about Dad. Nights were the hardest for Mom. I think our piling in bed with her the first couple of months helped her. It sure helped me."

Jayton's experience reminds me of a rather light-hearted story on the surface, but one with profound significance and implications for the power of touch. A mother put her young son to bed, but he ran from his room, crying out in fear. Trying to calm the frantic boy, she promised, "Jesus is with you. He will take care of you." The little boy quickly responded, "But Mom, I want someone with me in the dark who has skin I can feel!"

Another situation in which touch was a powerful source of comfort involves the death of a family's pet. The father had been in an accident, paralyzing him from the neck down. For an extended time, he was in a hospital in another city. While his wife accompanied him to the hospital, one set of grandparents stayed with their four children. The children seemed to do pretty well throughout the uncertain tension-filled days. After the mother returned home and the grandparents were leaving, everyone gathered around the driveway, telling the grandparents good-bye. As they drove away, the family dog ran under one of the car wheels. The dog died instantly. At that awful moment, the children exploded into hysterics. They had reacted calmly to their father's tragedy—they were too young to comprehend the implications of his paralysis. However, they did understand that their beloved family pet was dead, for their once lively, friendly, furry little dog lay limp and lifeless on the street. The person telling me about this calamity said neighbors each held a screaming, sobbing child until the ravaging emotions were nearly all poured out. The holding close gave more reassurance, more security than any attempted explanations or reasoning.

Not only do children need special reassurance in grief situations, they can also give comfort to others through hugs or other appropriate gestures of touch. In his delightful book, *Just a Touch of Nearness*, Fred Bauer tells this story:

> I once heard about the tragic traffic death of a young child. A speeding car had struck Nancy, just six years old. Her parents were devastated. So were her schoolmates, especially Joyce, Nancy's closest friend.

As soon as Joyce heard the news about Nancy, she wanted to run to her friend's house. However, Joyce's mother thought it would be too upsetting for their daughter and for Nancy's parents. "Daddy and you and I will go to the funeral," she consoled. "You can see Nancy's parents there." Nevertheless, a tearful Joyce insisted that she must see them immediately.

What worried Joyce's mother was what she herself might say to the grieving parents. Finally, reluctantly, she agreed to take her daughter to Nancy's house. When they arrived, Joyce ran to her lost friend's mother, climbed up on her lap, and threw her arms around her. Wordlessly, the two of them cried out their mutual hurt.

No one who came to say, "I'm sorry," said it better than Joyce.[11]

Hugs, a warm embrace, or a handclasp can say "I'm sorry" when words do not come easily. This was true in the case of Laura and her brother after their sister, Linda, was murdered by Linda's estranged husband. Linda was a young woman who loved everyone, and everyone loved back—except, of course, her estranged husband. The shock of this senseless death, according to Laura, was almost impossible to believe, much less survive.

The close-knit family clung even more tenaciously to each other. However, as so often is the case, words were inadequate to express the feelings churning around in the hearts and minds of the surviving relatives. Sometime after the heinous murder, Laura was filled with unexpressed feelings. So she put some of her emotions onto paper and sent a letter to her brother, telling him how she loved him. Since they no longer had Linda, Laura told him how she hoped they could become closer. Laura also told her brother something like this: "I also want my children to get to know you." Laura shared with me how she and her brother were both at their parents' home soon after she had sent that letter. Laura's brother said nothing about the letter but gave her an understanding hug—an embrace that transcended mere words.

The Touch That Hurts

Mary Evelyn, a friend of mine for over twenty-five years, said she could still remember some helpful hugs she had after her thirty-seven-year-old husband was killed in a plane crash, but she also remembers some that were not so helpful. Along with her recollections of touch and its healing power, she shared some myths she became aware of during her recovery. "First," she said, "some people thought if they were too sympathetic with me that I'd wallow in my grief indefinitely." She added an emphatic "Not so!" Then she explained, "People who let me grieve, giving me hugs, wiping away my tears, kissing my forehead . . . these all were like conduits of caring and concern helping get the grief out of my system.

"Another myth," continued Mary Evelyn, "was thinking that cheerfulness would automatically lighten my load and brighten my spirits." She elaborated how people would pat her on the shoulder, saying flippantly, "Cheer up! You'll get over it." Mary Evelyn said this kind of gaiety was hollow and false, making her feel even more despondent. A pat on the shoulder, she said, meant a lot more when someone said something more realistic to go along with it—for example, "I know you feel blue right now. But one of these days you'll find you aren't always thinking of your loss." Alternatively, something like this might be helpful, "There'll be better days ahead, and you'll start enjoying life most of the time. What could I do right now to encourage you?

"Furthermore," continued Mary Evelyn, "some people thought if I truly loved Dave, I should keep on grieving and never finish my grief." She explained how several people upon seeing her even a year after her husband's death would change to their most sorrowful expression, put their arms around her, and in their woebegone tone of voice say some doleful condolence. "In those instances," says Mary Evelyn, "I wanted to throw their arms off me! Their hugs hurt more than helped."

Another myth Mary Evelyn said that she became aware of has to do with over-idealization of the dead person. "People would put their arms benevolently around me," explained Mary Evelyn, "and patronizingly say something like, 'Dave was such a great guy.' I know they thought their comments would help me."

"The truth of the matter," says Mary Evelyn, "is that everyone knew Dave was a negative, moody, self-centered person who cared little about anyone but himself—and me—in that order." Mary Evelyn explained that no hug and no comment would have been better than overstating Dave's goodness. "Or maybe no comment and just a good hug or handclasp," she added.

Mary Evelyn's analysis of hugs and comments—how they must be realistic as well as sensitive—brings to mind a film I used to show in my marriage and family relationships course at the University of Nebraska. The film, called "What Man Shall Live and Not See Death," showed Elisabeth Kübler-Ross interviewing dying patients. One was a mother with a grown son and an eleven-year-old daughter. The mother said something like this as Elisabeth Kübler-Ross sat by her bed, tenderly holding her hand:

> I don't worry about my son. He's nearly grown, but I do worry about my daughter. She's so young. I want so much to live to help her grow up. You ask

what hurts? That's what hurts, knowing I won't get to help her grow up. And you know what else hurts? All these visitors coming in, bringing me all these get-well cards when we all know I am not going to get well and trying to tell me to cheer up as they pat me on the head. Then they start talking about their vacation plans and all the fun times they're planning this summer . . . and I know I probably will be gone by then.

This real-life account, like so many others, emphasizes the importance of being sensitive to what is going on in the life of anyone we're talking to; and then our comments and our gestures—hugs, handclasps, kisses, and others—will be more in tune with what that person needs at that moment.

Expressing Forgiveness

In spite of Darrell's pain-wracked heart, he knew what he needed to do. He knew he must go to see Beth and tell her that neither he, nor his wife, nor his daughter blamed her for his grandson Christopher's death. Beth babysat Chris—as his family affectionately called him—while his mother, Sylvia, worked. Beth had a child about Chris' age, and the two toddlers kept Beth busy. Going to the basement for something, Beth made certain she latched the door. Evidently wanting to follow her, Chris managed to open the door. He then toppled from the landing of the stairs to the hard concrete basement floor below, hitting headfirst. Christopher's death devastated Beth—she felt solely responsible.

Several years after this tragedy, Darrell and I met on the University of Nebraska campus. When I asked him how he managed to think about going to Beth when his own emotions were so shattered over his grandson's death, he said, "I don't know now. I just knew I must. I felt so sorry for her. I could just imagine if I had been in her place." Darrell did not tell me anything about his visit with Beth, but I heard from some of Beth's friends how he went to Beth's house and, in spite of his large six-foot-plus frame, he ever so tenderly put his arm around her and said, "We don't blame you and we don't want you to blame yourself." Later Beth told her friends, "Darrell's courage to come see me and to say what he did—and to hug me—helped me know they didn't hate me." This experience is like so many others in which blame for a death so easily could be placed on one person, but forgiveness prevailed rather than faultfinding.

Saying Good-bye

Remembering how a hug and well-chosen words helped in Darrell's situation reminds me of an experience I had when I was working in Swaziland, a beautiful rural kingdom surrounded by South Africa. In one of our village visits, I heard heartrending cries—low mournful sobs alternating with loud wailing. As we walked closer to a clump of trees, we saw a woman, cradling a baby in her arms and swaying back and forth, as she made those sad sounds. "Her baby must be very sick," I remember commenting. "No," answered our host, "her baby is dead." Part of the grief ritual includes holding the dead person for as long as wanted or until the loved one can say good-bye, our host explained.

That touching scenario brings back yet another memory from a few years earlier when the baby of some church friends died. The nurses briskly ushered the mother and father out of the room where the dead baby was, and as quickly as possible they also whisked away the baby. Years afterwards the mother said, "I've had this feeling all these years that I never got to hold my baby and to say good-bye to him." I have often thought how we overprotect against death, but trying to shield people against death sometimes actually causes more long-lasting hurt. The wisdom of those African villagers is sorely needed around the world!

The priest co-officiating at the services for my sister and brother-in-law did something that was akin to the African mother holding her dead baby until she was able to turn his body over to others for the burial. Father Juan had everyone in the immediate family encircle the casket, Robert's parents and brothers and sisters around his and us around Janet's, each of us putting our hands on the casket. While we kept our hands in place, he talked about "giving up," "letting go," and "saying good-bye." Touching that cold metallic casket was not the same as being able to give the sweet, pretty Janet we all knew a big love-filled hug good-bye. But it helped.

What's Appropriate and Helpful?

Embraces and other appropriate form of touch, must be a natural expression of caring, neither forced nor affected. Shakespeare said it eloquently in these lines:

> The quality of mercy is not strained,
> It droppeth as the gentle rain from heaven.

When Harry Clayton's mother died, Harry remembers an act of mercy that truly was "as the gentle rain from heaven." People coming through the receiving line were saying the usual patent conventionalities to Harry's stepfather: "At least she didn't suffer long," "She looked so natural," and so on. As Harry's stepfather bowed in grief, a soft-spoken friend raised on tiptoes, kissed him on the top of the head, said with heartfelt sincerity, "God bless you," and moved slowly on through the line.

Some people are more receptive than others are to expressions of sympathy. Granted, we all need to be sensitive to what will help the bereaved—not solely what will make us feel better for having done or said it. I remember one tough-talking, rough-acting fellow in our church several years ago. He was a good man morally, but his message—in words and body language—was clear: "I am strong, and I don't need anyone."

When his wife died, Paul's Achilles' heel was struck. Few people knew it, for they could not see through the tough exterior, the false front. A friend who understood people better than most psychiatrists do went to Paul, talked a while and then, getting up to leave, put his hand on Paul's head, pulling it gently to his own shoulder, and said, "You're a tough man—but you loved Mae and you have tears inside you. When you need a shoulder to cry on, I'd count it a privilege if you'd use mine." With that embrace and invitation, the friend left. Paul accepted that offer—many times. This experience shows how touch transcends human facades and how even the strongest need it. A bit of doggerel in the official guide to the London Zoo, of all places, makes this point:

> The rhino's skin is thick and tough,
> And yet this skin is soft enough
> that even rhinos always sense
> A love enormous and intense!

In a more serious vein, Ernest Hemingway wrote, "Life breaks us all and afterwards many are strong at the broken places." Lee Stillwell says she has found special meaning in these familiar words since both parents and her only two brothers died in a plane crash in Illinois years ago. "I was twenty years old, in my third year of college, had been married only three months, and I still was very close to my parents and brothers," explains Lee.

"At first I simply couldn't believe it—nothing this horrible could possibly happen to anyone—much less to me. I truly was 'broken.' My grief defied words—what could anyone say that would ease the razor-sharp pain?

"What helped most of all, at first," Lee recalls, "was my husband. I leaned on Vern, and I leaned hard—literally and figuratively. He would patiently hold me while I cried and questioned 'Why my family? Why my entire family?'" Continues Lee, "Vern understood my hopeless bewilderment somewhat, for his brother had died in Vietnam. My kind husband, wise beyond his years, kept his psychological, compassionate antennae out—moving closer to me at times, moving away, giving me room at other times.

"Out of my experience," says Lee, "I learned that helping the heartbroken cannot be reduced to simple rules but requires being very sensitive to what the person is feeling and needing at the moment. Surviving this tragedy also made me understand more fully the words of Shakespeare, 'We are in God's hands.'" Lee concludes, "I also learned that while words sometime fail, hugs or other forms of appropriate touch nearly always help."

Another example of the healing power of touch took place after a terrible car wreck killed my niece's fiancé. Viki, my brother's daughter, says that compassionate embraces and well-timed handclasps held her up—undergirding her both physically and emotionally. Viki recalls her feelings the last few days before Larry's death that ill-fated summer years ago—the fun-filled delight as she shopped for matching shirts for Larry and her to wear to the state fair in Albuquerque, New Mexico; the encouragement when Larry called her to insist she enroll in a computer course; and the joy as she looked forward to their January wedding date.

Viki's happiness had also suffered other dark, shadowy days. An automobile collision claimed the life of her mother when Viki was eleven. As Viki put it, "You never completely get over your mother's death." However, Viki had coped fairly well.

But nothing could have prepared Viki for this news: "Larry has been killed in a car wreck." The details of the collision were unclear. Larry was south of Albuquerque, driving home from work for the weekend. An oncoming car crossed over the centerline, hitting Larry's pickup head-on. The horrific impact killed both drivers.

Not only were the facts surrounding the death a blur, so was everything else, says Viki. She relates how her father put his arm around her as he told her that Larry had been killed. Then she remembers crying out, "It's not true. It has to be a mistake." Viki's world was spinning out of control again. Then her dad cradled her in his arms and said, "I'm sorry, it is true."

My brother knew the cruel shock and the crushing agony of losing someone you love. Bill was actually my half brother. His mother died when he was too young to remember her. His father (and my father) died when Bill was six. Then Bill's wife (Viki's mother) was killed in a car wreck when she was only thirty-four. Says Viki, "I knew Dad understood what I was going through. He held me, and we wept together.

"Looking back, I realize how fortunate I was," Viki says now. "Larry's family was also supportive. Even though they were hurting too, they reached out to me." Viki adds, "Larry's mother held my hand all through the funeral."

Steadying hugs, embraces, and outstretched hands for weeks, says Viki, helped and gave her courage to face life once more. Viki is now happily married to a kind, thoughtful individual, Walter, and they have two children—and grandchildren. Viki knows the pain of losing special people in her life—but those losses, she says, make her appreciate her husband and their two dear children even more. Viki says simply, "Hugs helped a lot."

No doubt, Viki and countless others who found consolation for their grief in the comforting arms of friends and family would agree with this brief but profound statement:

A hug is a prayer without words.

*S*tep 5
∽

*W*rite a *N*ote
Words work a miracle.

"*I* am sorry." "I am praying for you." "I am so sorry." "God be with you." Hundreds of individuals walked slowly and sadly by us after the services for my sister and her husband, whose short lives had been snuffed out by a drunk driver. All took their turns in the somber procession, saying brief, heartfelt utterances, sharing our unbearable grief. What more could they say? These tragic deaths were so sudden, so senseless. At that time we all were too stunned to comprehend any more.

Then the cards and notes started arriving. If any words help heal the hurting any more than spoken words, they are the wonderful words written in a note. Sincere words recorded on paper give the grieving person something to look at, to read over and over again. They are tangible, something to hold onto when all other moorings have been ripped away.

Suggestions for What to Write

Notes do not have to be long, eloquent, or penned in beautiful quill-scrolled calligraphy. Just a sincere expression of love and caring written in your own everyday handwriting will help comfort those who grieve! The same words of caring poured out at my sister and brother-in-law's funeral work well in writing. Something like the following might also be appropriate:

"I am sorry about your loss."
"I will be praying for you."
"I love you and will be thinking about you during these days."

Mention Admirable Qualities

A few additional sentences may add to the comforting power of the written word. You might, for example, mention some admirable qualities of the deceased. Julie, one of my most likable and conscientious students, was riding her bike through an intersection on her way from the university campus to a nearby store when she was struck by a concrete truck. She died several days later without ever regaining consciousness. Julie's parents received numerous cards and notes, and they recalled a particularly thoughtful message from one of Julie's teachers, Professor Dorcas Cavett, mother of Dick Cavett. "She wrote us," June says, "how much she had enjoyed having Julie in class and what a pleasure it was to know her, how cheerful and considerate Julie was and how much others liked her. We knew Julie was special, and it eased our misery for others to also remember her that way—and to take the time and make the effort to tell us so."

Some of the cards that people sent me after my grandfather died also mentioned some of his praiseworthy traits. Since my father died when I was a baby, my grandfather and I developed a special bond. Even though he lived to be nearly ninety, we did not suffer from a generation gap. After he died, the notes and cards people sent were a warm reminder of what we meant to each other.

One person simply wrote, "You were special to your grandfather." Another mentioned his lively sense of humor and his loyalty to his friends. One of my high school friends who especially enjoyed my grandfather wrote, "I'll always cherish the good talks we had with Granddad (she also called him Granddad). He always had time for us." I will always cherish these short personal notes.

After a brief illness, Jack Bond, a nationally recognized chemist, died. Edith, his widow, remembers one note in particular in which a friend wrote about her husband's fine qualities. It came from William Hillis, MD, at the time a noted researcher at Johns Hopkins University in Baltimore. "I loved Jack," he wrote. "He was such a wonderful person—and, of course, a great chemist. I will have a difficult time returning to Baylor University, knowing that Jack is no longer there."

Describe Valuable Contributions

Notes which briefly describe a valuable contribution the deceased person made during his or her lifetime may help ease the pain of losing that person. One of my best friends died December 25, decades ago. She threw herself into everything she did with great zest and compassion for others. After her death, her husband shared with me how consoling the notes were, especially those that said things like, "She touched so many people with her kindness and thoughtfulness" and "She was such a wonderful mother." These kinds of brief notes helped heal the hurt at the time, and they have become even more meaningful to the children as they grow older.

Another example of how notes can be comforting involves Dan, who died in a boating accident. Dan was a pillar in the community and a ready helper in church programs and activities. His wife, Sally, said that cards remarking about Dan's willingness to help with projects making life better for others were a great consolation to her. We know, of course, that all people who die are neither spiritual giants nor great workers in the community. Generally though all people have some admirable traits, and pointing these out in a note is a step toward helping heal the hurt their loved ones are experiencing.

Notes do not always have to be extremely serious and solemn to help comfort those who grieve. One friend shared with me a note she received soon after her husband of more than thirty years died. The note went something like this: "I know you can't laugh now, but I hope you can soon start remembering and enjoying the good times and the funny things that happened during the thirty years you and Jim shared. You have so many precious memories to cherish." The note continued, "One I'll always keep tucked in my mental scrapbook is the time Jim had been hunting and with his tender heart brought home a mongrel dog he'd found wandering along the highway. Covered with burrs and stickers, the dog was miserable. Jim just knew you'd help him cut them out—and you did."

Express Gratitude

Notes expressing gratitude can also lessen the pain. A friend whose mother died said this note from one of her mother's co-workers helped her: "I am thankful I got to know your mother. She was always so helpful to me in our work." Another person sent a similar note: "I am grateful for the friendship we shared. I'll miss her."

Offer Specific Help

Offers to help in some specific way can also encourage the disheartened. If you are willing, for example, for sorrow-stricken persons to call you on the telephone when they need someone to talk to, write a note telling them so. Then call them occasionally to show you really mean it. A friend I worked with wrote this note after my sister and brother-in-law were killed: "If you ever need to talk, I am a good listener."

Other offers may be a little more specific, like "Call me when you need to go to the grocery store. I'll be glad to go with you." Or "I'd love to drive your children to school or pick them up. Just let me know when." After an elderly man in our church died, I wrote a short note to the widow, offering my help and my husband's: "Next time your car needs gas and cleaning up, let us know. We're pretty good at that sort of thing." She seemed pleased, and she took us up on the offer.

The husband of Jan, one of the members of a weekly painting class I was in for a year or so, died. Jan had commented several times that painting was her "therapy," and she indeed did seem to enjoy the entire evening of painting and talking. After her husband's death, one of the class members wrote Jan this note: "When you are ready to paint again, let me know. I'd love to come by and give you a ride." Jan accepted the offer, commenting how much easier that ride with a friend made rejoining the group rather than coming by herself.

The father of one of a teacher's students died. Since the teacher's father had also died when she was young, she knew some of the turmoil her student was undoubtedly going through. She wrote a note to the student something like, "I am so sorry about your father. My father died when I was about your age, so I may be able to help you. Want to talk sometime?"

Notes to Children

In *Triumph Over Tears*, a book subtitled *How to Help a Widow*, Mary Brite offers a suggestion if the widow's children know you fairly well and are old enough to understand and to read. She says you might write a note to them something like this, "I am thinking about you as you adjust to a new life without your father" or, "I expect you have a lot of questions you would like to ask somebody. I have time and am willing to listen. Please feel free to call me or come over some time."

As discussed earlier, listening is a good way to help any grieving person. However, children may need a little more encouragement to talk. Mary Brite says you might suggest in a note—when appropriate and in your own words—that children:

- Ask questions.
- Talk to a teacher, counselor, minister, doctor, or almost anyone with whom he or she would be comfortable talking about feelings.
- Try to abide by the rules of the house, even if father is not there to enforce them or mother is too upset to notice.
- Tell mother "I love you."
- Realize mother's feelings will get better.
- Realize that his or her own feelings will improve.[1]

Based on her own experience and that of numerous other widows, Mary Brite also suggests that short notes might let the child know that it is normal to:

- Be afraid if mother is ill. (Help the child realize that

mother won't die right away just because father died.)

- Feel ashamed about the loss of father. (Let him or her know that you and others don't blame the child in any way. Perhaps you will want to verbalize the idea that it is not the child's fault.)

- Feel guilty if he or she wished father dead at some time. (Assure the child that father didn't die because the child wished it—and the child is not to worry about it.)[2]

Short notes might also let the child know that it is normal:

- To laugh.
- To cry.
- To hurt.
- To have nightmares.
- To question "Why?"
- To wonder "Why me?"
- To be temporarily mad at God.
- To be bitter.
- To hate someone connected with the death for a while.
- To be upset with father for leaving child and mother.
- To be guilty about something said or done to a missing parent.[3]

Mary Brite also emphasizes that it is generally helpful to let the child know in notes or in person that it is all right to have fun, to go on living, and to enjoy daily events when at all possible. Mary Brite, who had four young children when a plane crash killed her husband, suggests telling the children or any grieving person either in a note or in person that facing the finality of a father's death—or the death of anyone—takes time.

Children are often inadvertently ignored at the death of a parent or other loved one or friend. Notes or cards sent to the family are generally addressed to the entire family, and the child or children rarely read them. Thus, notes written specifically to a child may truly work a miracle in helping heal the hurt of losing a loved one.

Selected Writings, Poems, and Quotes

Carefully selected writings, poems, quotes, and other great literature can also be consoling to the bereaved. The Bible, of course, is a good source of such comfort. As the inspired word of God, Scriptures have proven down through the ages to be comforting. When my sister was killed, for example, one of my friends wrote simply, "My prayer for you is a verse which meant a lot to me when my daughter died: 'Cast your burden upon the Lord, and He will sustain you.'" (Psalm 55:22, *New American Standard*)

Bible Verses

One of the all-time favorites of mourners throughout the centuries is the Twenty-third Psalm:

"The Lord is my shepherd; I shall not want.

He maketh me to lie down in green pastures: he leadeth me beside the still waters.

He restoreth my soul: he leadeth me in the paths of righteousness for his name's sake.

Yea, though I walk through the valley of the shadow of death, I will fear no evil: for thou art with me; thy rod and thy staff they comfort me.

Thou preparest a table before me in the presence of mine enemies: thou annointest my head with oil; my cup runneth over.

Surely goodness and mercy shall follow me all the days of my life: and I will dwell in the house of the Lord forever."

Sending a copy of the beautiful Twenty-third Psalm along with a handwritten note may be especially comforting and encouraging. Other Bible Scriptures like the following, included with a personal note, may also be helpful and healing:

"God is our refuge and strength, a very present help in trouble." (Psalm 46:1)

"He heals the brokenhearted." (Psalm 147:3, *Revised Standard Version*)

"He hath said, I will never leave thee, nor forsake thee." (Hebrews 13:5)

"Hope we have as an anchor of the soul, both sure and steadfast." (Hebrews 6:19)

"Let not your hearts be troubled; believe in God." (John 14:1, *Revised Standard Version*)

"Fear not, for I am with you, be not dismayed, for I am your God; I will strengthen you, I will help you, I will uphold you." (Isaiah, 41:10, *Revised Standard Version*)

"The eternal God is thy refuge, and underneath are the everlasting arms." (Deuteronomy 33:27)

"Trust in the Lord with all thine heart; and lean not unto thine own understanding. In all thy ways acknowledge him, and he shall direct thy paths."

(Proverbs 3:5, 6)

"When I pray, you answer me, and encourage me by giving me the strength I need." (Psalm 138:3, *The Living Bible*)

"Be strong and of a good courage, fear not for the Lord thy God, he it is that doth go with thee; he will not fail thee, nor forsake thee." (Deuteronomy 31:6)

A friend shared a story with me that shows how a caring person could use a Scripture to help a bereaved person. John, a man in his fifties, had outlived two wives—one died in a car wreck and the other of cancer. Only months after John's second wife died, as the story was told to me, the neighbor's wife died. The neighbor returned home one day to find a note tacked to his door. Taking the words from Second Corinthians, John had written something like this: "What a wonderful God we have—He is the source of every mercy, and the one who so wonderfully comforts and strengthens us in our hardships and trials. And why does He do this? So that when others are troubled, needing our sympathy and encouragement, we can pass on to them this same help and comfort God has given us." (1:3-4, *The Living Bible*)

A relative of mine passed on some comfort to me after one of my favorite aunts died. Aunt Nora truly tried to live out her Christian convictions. She was very industrious in her home, and she was a dedicated elementary school teacher for forty years, loving every minute of it! Proverbs 31 did indeed describe her, and that was the passage of Scripture the pastor read at the service. Later a thoughtful note arrived, reminding me of my aunt's virtues and how that passage was genuinely appropriate—and how my aunt truly cared for me. That note still means a lot to me.

Soon after the death of a loved one, grieving persons generally read the notes, letters, and cards and register in their minds who sent them. That helps. However, after the funeral is over and everyone has gone home, these personal messages seem to take on deeper meaning and really help comfort those who grieve. That's when the bereaved take the time to read the words and comprehend the messages.

Poetry

Even people who may not have cared a great deal for poetry in the past admit that some of the verses sent to them were quite meaningful. Others who have always enjoyed poetry are especially thankful for the messages sent to them in verse. Just as with any gift or thoughtful gesture, what would be meaningful to the grieving person must be the criterion for selection. Poems which have provided encouragement and comfort to others include "Thanatopsis" by William Cullen Bryant; "Revisitation" by Anne Morrow Lindbergh; "The Dying Need But Little Dear" by Emily Dickinson; "To an Athlete Dying Young" by A.E. Housman; "Spring and Fall: To a Young Child" by Gerard M. Hopkins; and "Elegy Written in a Country Churchyard" by Thomas Gray.

After Mary Christensen's nineteen-year-old daughter was killed in a motorcycle-car collision in Connecticut, she found special solace in a collection of poems a friend gave her. Mary says, "The poems put into words all the emotions I was feeling and helped me to better understand the meaning of everything I was going through." One of Mary's favorites in the collection was by Emily Dickinson:

> The bustle in the house
> The Morning after death
> Is solemnest of industries
> Enacted upon Earth—
> The Sweeping up the heart

And putting love away
We shall not want to use again
Until eternity.

An elderly widow shared with me a poem (the author unknown), explaining that a friend copied it from a wooden decoupage at the home of another widow. These widows always pass this poem on with the hope that it will offer comfort to a new widow just as it spoke to them in their own time of grief. Here it is, simple in form but beautiful in thought:

The Lights are out
In the mansion of clay;
The curtains are drawn,
For the dweller's away;
He silently slipped
O'er the threshold by night,
To make his abode
In the City of Light.

One rancher in western Nebraska said this poem was especially touching to him. A neighboring ranch family sent it to him, copying it from a card they had received years before when the grandmother died.

In the Loss of Your Loved One

A chapter completed,
A page turned,
A life well-lived,
A rest well-earned.
May you find peace in

the knowledge that your
loved one has completed but
one chapter in the Book of
Eternal Life.

Helen Steiner Rice has a special gift of expressing emotions felt by grieving persons. Two of my favorite books of hers are *The Beloved Poetry of Helen Steiner Rice* and *Expressions of Comfort.*

Poems selected with the person and specific situation in mind are the most comforting. Howard and Evelyn Handyside's loss certainly demonstrated this. Their fourteen-year-old son drowned in Lake St. Clair, Michigan, during Easter holidays. Someone sent them Edgar A. Guest's poem, "To All Parents." They said it really helped. They in turn send a copy to anyone they hear about whose child has died. Here is the response from one set of distraught parents who received a copy of the poem: "We returned to a very quiet home following the funeral, totally drained with nothing to hold onto—then found your poem in the mail. It was just what we needed and turned our thoughts from very negative ones to positive ones."

Generally, shorter poems are better than longer ones: the attention span of the grief-stricken is often short and fractured. Similarly, other writings, accompanied by a personal note, may be consoling and helpful. When my husband's brother was forty-four, he died of a brain tumor, leaving a wife, Sue, and four sons, ages eight to nineteen. Several different people gave the following inspirational writing to Sue. She says even today she reads "Footprints" and finds it comforting and encouraging:

One night a man had a dream. He dreamed
he was walking along the beach with the LORD.
Across the sky flashed scenes from his life. For each

scene, he noticed two sets of footprints in the sand: one belonging to him, and the other to the LORD.

When the last scene of his life flashed before him, he looked back at the footprints in the sand. He noticed that many times along the path of his life there was only one set of footprints. He also noticed that it happened at the very lowest and saddest times in his life.

This really bothered him and he questioned the LORD about it, "LORD, you said that once I decided to follow you, you'd walk with me all the way. But I have noticed that during the most troublesome times in my life, there is only one set of footprints. I don't understand why when I needed you most you would leave me."

The LORD replied, "My precious, precious child, I love you and I would never leave you. During your times of trial and suffering, when you see only one set of footprints, it was then that I carried you."

Songs

Down through the ages songs have comforted the heartbroken and soothed the hurt when a loved one dies. "Because He Lives" was a favorite song of my sister Janet. The lyrics of this song became even more poignant to me when a young couple sang this song at the funeral of Janet and her husband. Some of the words go like this:

> Because He lives, I can face tomorrow.
> Because He lives, all fear is gone.

Because I know He holds the future,
And life is worth the living
Just because He lives![4]

Two different people later wrote notes to us, referring to that song and how glad they were to hear its message at the funeral. One wrote something like "I'm glad you selected 'Because He Lives.' I hope you can have faith that because God lives, you truly can face tomorrow."

Another friend and I have had a long tradition of sharing thoughts from books we have read and enjoyed. Several years ago we enjoyed reading a book about Ethel Waters entitled *His Eye Is on the Sparrow*. Some time later my friend's husband passed away, and she was, of course, anxious and fearful about the future. I wrote her a simple note: "Remember the wonderful book, *His Eye Is on the Sparrow*, and how God was with Ethel Waters throughout the tragedies in her life? My prayer is that you will feel God's presence in these difficult days. And if I could put a song in your heart, it would be 'His Eye Is on the Sparrow'":

Let not your heart be troubled,
His tender word I hear,
And resting on His goodness,
I lose my doubts and fears,
Though by the path He leadeth,
But one step I may see:
His eye is on the sparrow,
And I know He watches me,
His eye is on the sparrow,
And I know He watches me.[5]

Phil Gately was an amiable twenty-three-year-old who had spent a good part of the day with his mother, father, and two sisters and their husbands on Mother's Day, 1978. With plans to return to his apartment in town, he pulled away from his parents' country home, perhaps happily thinking of the pleasant visit. Scarcely a mile away from his parents' house, he drove through an intersection he had routinely driven through for seven years. Someone else, evidently unfamiliar with the road, ran the stop sign, hitting Phil's pickup broadside. Phil hung onto life by a fragile thread for thirteen months before he died. At the funeral, the many friends and relatives sang "How Great Thou Art" by Stuart K. Hine. Having grown up in an orphanage herself, Mae Gately dearly loved Phil and her other children. The devoted and disconsolate mother mentioned later how much that song meant to her. She commented that she could understand even more Mary's agony, seeing her son, Jesus, die on the cross. Mae said that song helped soothe her own hurt. Overhearing Mae's comments, a friend later wrote a note to Mae, including the words of this hymn. When Mae died several years later, the friend's card with the words of "How Great Thou Art" written on it was found, well worn, in Mae's Bible.

Quotes

Personal notes that include quotes, selected with sensitivity and the specific person in mind, take a little extra time and thought, but the healing effect they may have on a grief-stricken friend is well worth the effort. Sources for short, comforting quotes are almost limitless. One delightful little book, full of words of wisdom that will turn weakness into strength, is *When Sorrow Comes*. Here is a passage from that book I have shared with those in despair:

I wish I had a magic word to wipe away your tears!
I do not know any magic words, but I know a God who

can heal you and I commend Him to you. Remember, the door of death is the only door that leads to the Father's house. He will be waiting there to greet and welcome His children.[6]

Peter Marshall, the legendary Scottish chaplain of the United States Senate in the late 1940s, died at age forty-six. Uncanny as it seems, he was reported to have spoken words befitting his own eulogy: "The measure of a life, after all, is not its duration, but its donation." When the death of a younger person occurs, these words may be appropriately incorporated into a personal note.

Quotes included in notes do not have to be spoken by famous people. The main criterion is that the quote is something that helps soothe the hurt caused by the death of a loved one. A student was killed in a car wreck while on spring break from the university she was attending. My friend, a faculty sponsor of the girl's sorority, recalled how this vibrant young woman would tell other students, "Bloom where you are planted." My friend wrote a note to the student's mother and father. It went something like "Your daughter was such an encouragement to her friends. With wisdom far beyond her years, she often cheered them on, saying, 'Bloom where you are planted.'"

A young woman's husband was killed in a plane crash. They had been married only a short while. In her grief she was heard to say perhaps it would have been less painful if she had not loved her husband so much. One wise person wrote her a brief note, commenting that loving always assumes a risk of losing, and then she quoted Elizabeth Barrett Browning: "Unless you can swear for life or death, oh fear to call it loving."

My paternal grandfather loved great literature and could quote long passages. The fact that he was a large towering farmer planted in the windswept portion of Eastern New Mexico added to the delight of listening to him spill out the whole of William Cullen Bryant's "Thanatopsis" and portions from other great writers such as Shakespeare. Two of my grandfather's sons died early in life: one was my father, and one was a lad in his teens that had gone to Oklahoma to visit when he developed pneumonia and died. At the death of each of these sons and in his efforts to comfort other family members, I recall stories about his sharing quotes like this one from Charles Dickens:

> When death strikes down the innocent and young, a hundred virtues rise, in shapes of mercy, charity, and love, to walk the world and bless it. Of every tear that sorrowing mortals shed on such green graves some good is born, some gentler nature comes. In the Destroyer's steps there spring up bright creations that defy his power, and his dark path becomes a way of light to heaven.

The following quote attributed to Helen Keller could also be shared in a written note to mourners:

> We, the living, should not think of the dead because if they could speak to us, they would say: "Do not weep for me, earth was not my true country, I was an alien there; I am now at Home where every one comes in his turn."

Not until we have taken the step from life into eternity shall we understand the meaning of Browning's words: "On earth, the broken arc; in heaven, a perfect round."

A line from a letter Abraham Lincoln wrote to the parents of a fallen soldier would be consoling in a note to any grieving person: "May

God give you that consolation which is beyond all earthly power."

Articles

Articles on how to handle grief appear with some regularity in popular magazines. Sometimes it can be helpful to locate an appropriate article and send a copy to a bereaved friend or relative along with a brief note. Roma Weirich, of Austin, Texas, said that she was touched by the number of people who went to the trouble to send her copies of such articles after her husband, George, died in March of 1986. She admitted some of them were helpful, and some were not. Nevertheless, the thoughtful gesture always eased the hurt. *Reader's Digest* has published some excellent articles helpful to the grief-stricken. (Back issues can usually be found in public libraries.) In one such article (April, 1980), Ardis Whitman, who first lost her husband and then her only son, offers inspiration to others with "Six Special Powers of Prayer."

"Good-By, Grandma," a moving story by Ray Bradbury, the world-famous author of *The Martian Chronicles, Fahrenheit 451,* and other classics, was originally published in 1957 in *Dandelion Wine* and later in the July, 1983, *Reader's Digest.* In certain situations it could bring solace. "When I Lost My Husband" is another *Reader's Digest* article (March 1987) in which some hard-won advice about coping with bereavement is offered. A new widow would find it helpful.

"The Lesson of the Cliff," another encouraging article, appeared first in the July 14, 1985, *Parade* and later in the *Reader's Digest,* February 1986. In it Morton Hunt describes how as a young boy he and his friends climbed a sixty-foot cliff—a bristling near-vertical wall of jutting rocks, earth slides, scraggly bushes, and slender saplings. The others scrambled down, but Morton froze in terror. As dark was approaching, his father came looking for him. His father wisely guided him down, telling him to take "just one step at a time." The author then goes on to tell how this lesson helped him through some traumatic adult experiences. Most grievers will be able to see this poignant story's application in their own situation—that is, to face the myriad adjustments a death creates, take "just one step at a time."

Prayers

Prayers in notes and references to prayers can be encouraging and help heal the hurt, according to many who have suffered the death of a loved one. One of the most touching notes Sharla received after her son and husband died in a fiery car wreck was from a friend at church. The friend wrote: "I will be praying for you every morning at 7:00." Another note included this prayer: "When the joy of living is lost, O God, and life becomes a long weariness, kindle again the light that has failed, and the love that will not let me go."

Gladys was a dear woman in her mid-fifties: Both parents had recently died, one of her three adult children was killed in Vietnam, and her husband died after a long, drawn-out battle with cancer. A friend sent her a small booklet entitled *Wonderful Promises*, by Norman Vincent Peale. Gladys said the prayers in this booklet were most uplifting, with this one being her favorite:

> Lord, when sometimes my life in this world seems too much to bear, help me to claim Your wonderful promise of victory over tears, death, sorrow and pain. I thank you that all things are made new through You and that I will share in Your kingdom.[7]

One man whose wife had been murdered received a prayer from a couple who said the prayer had helped them after their daughter was tortured and killed, for it voiced what they were feeling but could not say. They hoped it would be helpful to the new widower. Sharing this prayer might be helpful at the death of other loved ones:

> I am empty, Father. I am bitter, even toward You. I grieve, not only for the one I have lost, but for the loving part of myself that seems to have died as well. You, Who have at other times brought the dead back to life, revive my dead ability to love, to be close, to care about this world and those I know. I believe, I insist, that You can heal this mortal wound.[8]

Before her death in 1983 Corrie ten Boom wrote of her experiences in concentration camps in World War II, and she traveled all over the world spreading her message of love and reconciliation. Corrie, her sister, and her father had been arrested for sheltering Jews in their home. Just as God's love empowered her to survive the awful indignities of the concentration camp and provided her a hiding place, so will God's love sustain the person imprisoned in grief and despair over the death of a loved one. Sharing Corrie ten Boom's short but powerful prayer "The Hiding Place" with a grief-stricken person who is already familiar with Corrie's life could be meaningful:

> Thank you, Lord Jesus
> that you will be our hiding place,
> whatever happens.[9]

Cards

Commercial cards include many of the prayers, Scriptures, poems, and other quotes and ideas suggested in this chapter. No doubt, commercial cards can be quite helpful and healing. Without fail, however, grieving persons say that notes written with these commercial messages added to the feeling that the sender cared deeply and personally about the grief-stricken person. Adding at least a line or two of your own expression of love and concern simply strengthens the comforting power of the note. You can add something as simple as "This is my prayer for you" or "The message in this card captures my thoughts for you."

Another suggestion when sending a commercial card is to read the message carefully, making sure it sends the idea you want the bereaved person to receive. Also try to select a message that is consistent with the mourning person's religious beliefs. Being sensitive to a person's religious convictions will make the message more helpful and healing. That is the whole point of sending a note or card.

Being aware of the visual impact of a card is also important. Choose a card with a picture you feel will be pleasing to the grief-stricken person. Martha Jackson said many of the cards she received upon her mother's death had pictures of roses on them. Martha's mother loved all flowers but was particularly fond of roses. These cards were especially meaningful to Martha.

Fear of Writing the Wrong Thing

Many people are hesitant to say anything or to write a note to the grieving person for fear they will say or write the wrong thing. Over concern, admits Christian psychologist G. B. Dunning, may intimidate people so they do nothing. Remembering the sage advice in First Peter 4:8 may be helpful: "Most important of all, continue to show deep love for each other, for love makes up for many of your faults." (*The Living Bible*) With a little thought and motivated by love, continues Dr. Dunning, "people can say something that is consoling.

To say nothing is generally the most hurtful recourse." Even poets have recognized this wisdom. William Blake put it this way in "On Another's Sorrow":

> Can I see another's woe,
> And not be in sorrow too?
> Can I see another's grief,
> And not seek for kind relief?[10]

Advice That Hurts vs. Advice That Helps

On the other hand, avoid giving authoritative-sounding advice, say many who have lost loved ones. "It seems like everyone wants to help by telling you what to do and what not to do," admitted one widower. "Some say 'Go on a cruise,' while others insist 'Stay home and get adjusted to your new life.'" One bit of advice that did indeed seem wise was given to a widow. A friend wrote to her:

> Everyone will be giving you advice, telling you what to do and what not to do. What worked best for me after Jack died was just to do what I felt was right for me. I would advise against making any major decisions right away.

Another friend wrote simply, "The best advice I can give is 'Beware of advice.'" Some more good advice might be not to carry this advice too far, for many people have had experiences that may be helpful to the newly saddened person. For example, one person said a note like this provided excellent advice: "When my child was killed, I thought it was the end of the world, and I know you must feel this way too. It helped me to try to begin each day with positive thoughts, things I was thankful for and the good memories I had of Jamie."

Another person, a widower, wrote to a grieving friend whose wife had also died: "It helped me when Sara died to do the best I could to get through each day and not to think I had to plan out my entire future without her." Others who have received notes like these agree that advice is more helpful if based on the writer's own experience and shared more in the sense of "This worked for me, and it might help you."

Paul backed out of the driveway over his small two-year-old Tim—only seconds before he had seen Tim go into the kitchen door. His son died in his arms on the way to the hospital. Paul understandably was devastated. In cases like this, we often are especially unsure of what to say. The Golden Rule provides a good guideline: "Do unto others as you would have them do unto you." Try to put yourself in the place of the grieving person and consider what words would help your hurt. Paul said notes ministering to him went something like this: "Paul, please don't blame yourself, and don't think of the 'might-have-beens.' All of us who are parents know this could've happened to any one of us many times. We don't understand why this had to happen, but no one blames you, and you must not put heavy guilt on yourself. We love you."

Notes and Cards Throughout the Year

Sometimes people do not hear about a death until some time has passed. Then they often feel like it is too late to send a note or card. Most mourning people contend it is never too late to express love and concern. The survivor generally is still thinking about the dead loved one long after others assume he or she is fairly well adjusted. Virgie Ryon's husband died during the summer months while many of her friends were out-of-town. Virgie shared how letdown she felt when several people never said anything nor sent a card or note. In this case, a note several weeks or a month or so after the death indeed would have been helpful.

In fact, notes and cards throughout the first year may be encouraging. One widow describes another widow's reaction to the death of a husband:

> Then her shock melts away a small bit at a time and painful awareness comes slowly. The loneliness becomes a heavy binding chain. A time comes when emotions surface, reactions grow enormous, and she needs comforting friends. And that is about the time some acquaintance says, "I guess you have adjusted now!"[11]

Friends who want to comfort and to help someone handle grief need to remember that the first year is the hardest to get through. People of the Jewish faith recognize the importance of waiting until the first year is over to erect a permanent monument in memory of a loved one. They know the difficulty of living through that first year and that the first anniversary date brings fresh grief. Holidays, birthdays, weekends, and other special occasions can also be especially stressful. A brief but thoughtful note may give some sorely needed encouragement. A case in point: After the death of my brother-in-law—the brother-in-law with four young sons—my husband and other relatives sent cards not only on the boys' and their mother's birthdays but on other holidays, such as Mother's Day. There were also cards and calls on Father's Day, my brother-in-law's birthday, and the anniversary date of his death. "These made a big difference in getting through that first brutal year," my husband's widowed sister-in-law says.

Other Kinds of Notes

Other notes may need to be written after a death. When eighty-eight-year-old Katy Miller died, her two adult children saw each other for the first time since they had gathered seven years earlier for their father's funeral. Both had harbored ill feelings about the division of their father's belongings. In addition, there were other longstanding feelings of jealousy and malcontent. Linda had especially felt that her mother gave preferential treatment to her younger sister, Jean.

Linda seemed to grieve excessively over her mother's death. She could not sort out her feelings. She had always given her mother a lot of attention, and she had no regrets—she thought. Then she realized she had kept from her mother the most precious gift of all—that of adult children relating to each other in a mature, caring way. Linda wrote a letter to Jean that went something like this: "I am sorry I have been so selfish and self-centered through the years. Will you please forgive me?"

Jean responded positively—and Linda began working through her grief in a miraculously healing way. This story illustrates how notes must be personalized. They should be a reflection of what needs to be said, and they should be sensitive to the particular situation.

The written word has unbounded power to help the grief-stricken handle the anguish of losing a loved one. One Proverb says, "Like apples of gold in settings of silver, so is a word spoken at the right moment." (Proverbs 25:11, *Modern Language Bible*) Experience of grieving persons shows that this Proverb may well include "a word written at the right moment"—whether it is written one day after the death or later. Down through the years, my mother said the anniversary date of my father's death was always a difficult day for her. Remembering this, I sent her a card, timed to arrive on November 2, the fortieth anniversary of my father's death. It was one of those cheerful thinking-of-you cards. I then added a note: "Thanks for being a terrific mother through some tough times. I'll be thinking of you today." My mother was touched. She responded to the note in a way, I think, that speaks for all people who receive notes when a loved one dies and at any time thereafter. She said simply, "Thanks for remembering."

Step 6

Give a Gift
It's the thought that counts.

"*I* am in the habit of looking not so much to the nature of the gift as to the spirit in which it is offered." These words were spoken by Robert Louis Stevenson, one of the most-read adventure novelists of the late 1800s. (*Treasure Island* was my favorite book he wrote.) A line in the play, *Le Menter*, expressed this same thought about gifts in about 1642: "The manner of giving is worth more than the gift." These statements could apply quite specifically to gifts for the bereaved.

The Healing Power of a Thoughtful Gift

Gifts do not have to be expensive. The most touching gifts, in fact, may not cost much at all. The main consideration is that the gift is selected with the bereaved person in mind. What would be healing to one person may not be for another. In addition, the spirit in which the gift is given adds to its comforting power. Carefully selecting a gift and giving it in a thoughtful way can be a very healing step to take, for gifts are tangible reminders to the bereaved that someone cares.

Flowers

Down through the ages flowers have traditionally been used at rites of passage—weddings, funerals, and other special occasions, happy and sad. Flowers have historically been a gift that says, "I care." During the last few years, other ways of showing our concern have supplanted the prominent place flowers formerly had. Some people think flowers do not last, but I think they are very healing at the time, and grief-stricken people need that. At a recent funeral, for example, I overheard a heartbroken person whisper, "Aren't the flowers beautiful. A lot of people loved her." Flowers express what we are sometimes unable to say in words. That is, "I care." Irving Berlin captured the thought well in his song, "Say It with Flowers."

Lynda Manning, the teenage daughter of a friend of mine, died unexpectedly and suddenly while attending Mt. Lebanon, a church camp near Dallas, Texas. Lynda's mother, Lorita, said one unique gift, also an unusually meaningful one, was a beautiful long-stemmed rose selected by some special friends for Lynda's funeral. The rose was placed in Lynda's hands. Lorita said, "We were stunned by Lynda's death. We never would've thought of a rose for her. Lynda lived life as a beautiful gift, and that rose seemed to symbolize this thought."[1]

Another gesture, which may add a healing touch, is to offer after the service or at some other appropriate time to take some of the flowers to nursing homes or to shut-ins. After my father-in-law's death, for example, the house was overflowing with plants and flowers. When my mother-in-law had enjoyed them for several days, she commented, "These are beautiful. I just wish I could share them." We all realized

that Mrs. Chesser's home was too small for the numerous flowers that
caring friends and relatives had delivered there—but Dan McClung, a
long-time friend, was the one who had the perception and sensitivity
to say, "I'll be glad to take some of them to the nursing home if you'd
like." Word came back to Mrs. Chesser that her generous sharing
of the flowers touched the nursing home residents. In this case, the
flowers brought double comfort to Mrs. Chesser. What had happened
is expressed in these old familiar lines:

> Have you had a kindness shown?
> Pass it on.

You might consider giving a potted plant since it would be more
lasting. When my grandfather died, for instance, someone sent my
grandmother a beautiful heart-shaped philodendron. As this easy-
to-grow ivy flourished, my grandmother shared cuttings from it. She
enjoyed being able to do this, and the comfort from that one plant
was multiplied many times as she expressed her own caring to friends
and other members of the family—including me. Case in point: My
grandfather has been dead for many years, but I still have pleasant
memories of him when I look into my living room at a large planter of
ivy that came from that long-ago but thoughtful gift.

Many churches and temples welcome having floral
arrangements for the worship service with the program denoting
who gave the flowers and for what occasion. Jim Kagan was a quiet
man who went about doing good deeds for his friends and neighbors
with never a desire for payment or praise. Jim's widow shared with
me how a beautiful arrangement was provided for the Christmas
worship service the first Christmas after Jim died. The note in the
program said something like this:

The Christmas arrangement is in memory of Jim Kagan, who was a loyal friend. He truly believed and lived the spirit of this Scripture: "Then shall the King say unto them on his right hand, Come, ye blessed of my Father, inherit the kingdom prepared for you from the foundation of the world: For I was an hungered, and ye gave me meat: I was thirsty, and ye gave me drink: I was a stranger, and ye took me in: Naked and ye clothed me: I was sick, and ye visited me: I was in prison, and ye came unto me. Then shall the righteous answer him, saying, Lord, when saw we thee hungered, and fed thee? or thirsty, and gave thee drink? When saw we thee a stranger, and took thee in? or naked, and clothed thee? Or when saw we thee sick, or in prison, and came unto thee? And the King shall answer and say unto them, Verily I say unto you, Inasmuch as ye have done it unto one of the least of these my brothers, ye have done it unto me." (Matthew 25:34–40)

To indicate who had provided the beautiful floral arrangement and the tribute, the program was signed simply, "Jim's grateful friends." Jim's widow drew much comfort from that gift and gesture.

Food

Food has also been a traditional expression of caring and concern for the bereaved. Customs vary from community to community, from neighborhood to neighborhood, and even from family to family. You want to take into account the acceptable way of doing things, but nonetheless there are some considerations in making sure your gift of food is as helpful as you want it to be. You may wish to call the house, or even go by, to see if anyone is responsible for specific plans for food or particular meals. When Diane Mullens' relative died, for instance, friends who owned a restaurant catered several meals. Therefore, friends answering the phone asked others to bring food that the bereaved could eat at a later time.

Most people, of course, do not have friends who own a restaurant, but other plans may already be made for meals. Knowing these arrangements can help you think through what is best for you to do. Knowing the number of people who will be eating at the home and for how many meals or days may also help you make a wise decision of what to bring, how much, and when. This information cannot always be predicted, but usually an estimate can be made.

It has been my observation that an inordinate amount of the food is desserts. Pies, cakes, and other sweets are, of course, considered special, but sometimes a pot of homemade soup, some appetizing vegetables, or a bowl of fresh fruit would add a balancing touch to all the food.

Most people usually take food for midday or evening meals, but when Millie's husband died, several friends planned a simple but tasty breakfast for the morning of the funeral. One friend went by the bakery and arrived in Millie's kitchen with freshly-baked cinnamon rolls, another friend brought an egg-cheese dish straight from the oven, and another came with a large pitcher of orange juice. A friend who worked and couldn't be at Millie's home that morning took by a can of coffee and some attractive disposable dishes the evening before.

Later that afternoon, another friend, who worked outside the home and rarely cooked, brought several large containers of soft drinks along with some pretty plastic cups and small matching napkins. Recalls Millie, "Many people dropped in to see me but didn't stay for meals. Looking back, I can remember it gave me a good feeling to be able to offer them a cold soft drink."

Other considerations to make your gift of food as helpful as possible include putting the food in a disposable container so the bereaved does not have the later hassle of returning dishes. If you prefer to take your food in a dish that must be returned, be sure to label it with your name. A postage label with your name and address on it is handy to stick on the bottom of a dish. Taping over the label with transparent tape makes it waterproof. It is also a good idea to attach a note securely to the covering of the dish of food, telling what the food is, if it needs to be refrigerated, if it can be frozen for later use, what is needed in the way of final preparation for serving, and who brought it.

Often friends and relatives bring so much food at first that there is not enough room in the refrigerator or freezer for it all. On the other hand, sometimes there is not enough food or not an adequate variety for a complete meal. Friends would do well to check out what the food situation is and then act accordingly. Sometimes a gift of food for the bereaved is even more welcome a week or so after all the friends and relatives have gone home. Keep all these different ideas in mind so that your gift of food does what you want it to—that is, comfort those who grieve.

Books

Giving a carefully chosen book may also convey consideration to the bereaved and help comfort them. Several widows, for example, say as new widows they were given some helpful books, such as Shirley Reeser McNally's *When Husbands Die*. Because this book was such a meaningful gift to them, many of these widows have developed the practice of giving it or another book of this nature to newly widowed friends. Other helpful books for widows and widowers are *Thoughts for the Lonely Nights: A Conversation About Grief* by Doug Manning and Kathy Burns and *Experiencing Grief* by H. Norman Wright. Especially healing to parents whose child has died include *A Child Dies: A Portrait of Family Grief* by Joan Hagan Arnold and Penelope Buschman Gemma, *Tracks of a Fellow Struggler* by John Claypool, and *On Wings of Mourning* by Carol A. and William J. Rowley.

The titles of the following books indicate the loss for which they may be helpful as gifts: *Dying to Be Free: A Healing Guide for Families After Suicide* by Cobain and Jean Larch, *When a Friend Dies: A Book for Teens About Grieving and Healing* by Marilyn E. Gootmann and Pamela Eppeland, and *My Grandma Died: A Child's Story About Grief and Loss* by Lory Britain and Carol Deach.

A book that may be helpful after a miscarriage is *I Never Held You: A Book About Miscarriage, Healing, and Recovery* by Ellen M. DuBois. Another helpful book is *Death of a Dream* by Donna and Rodger Ewy. I wish these books had been available and given to me decades ago when I suffered two miscarriages. I realize now that I simply did not handle my grief very well. These books would have been about the most valuable gifts I ever received. In addition, *Stillborn: The Invisible Death* by John DeFrain and others is a very insightful book to help mothers and fathers cope with one of life's most wrenching heartbreaks—a stillborn baby. Rabbi Earl A. Grollman, a noted authority on grief and bereavement, said this about it: "One of the most outstanding books of the decade dealing with death, it is helpful; it is so human. It should be required reading for social scientists and bereaved people alike."[2] One father said, "A friend gave us this book. Kay and I read it together. It helped us more than anything."

Reading the book yourself or looking it over carefully is a must to ensure that you choose a book that is appropriate for your friend and one your friend would find meaningful. Consider the case of

Lynda Manning, my friend's daughter who died. Lynda was, among other accomplishments, an excellent runner. She was training, in fact, under an Olympic coach at the time of her death. Lorita, Lynda's mother, said several thoughtful friends gave her books after Lynda's death, but *Sandy: A Heart for God* by Leighton Ford comforted her most. Sandy was the son of Leighton Ford, a brother-in-law of Billy Graham. Also a runner, Sandy died when he was twenty-one. This book is the father's story of his son's life and his death. My friend says, "I could identify with so much in the book about Sandy. The subtitle, *A Heart for God*, for instance, reminded me of something Lynda had written in her spiritual notebook, which I was reading shortly after her death. She had written, 'All my life I will always love God.'" Concludes Lorita, "That book was a very special gift."

After my twenty-year-old sister and brother-in-law were killed, a friend gave me *The Courage to Grieve* by Judy Tatelbaum. It is a book written by a woman whose twenty-year-old brother was killed, but if offers sensible insights to anyone whose loved one has died. Dr. W J Wimpee, chaplain at Baylor University at the time, gave me a small book called *Good Grief* by Granger E. Westberg. This book is also excellent—concise enough that a grieving person's short attention span can handle it, and it discusses some of the piercing emotions and issues with which grief-stricken people frequently struggle.

Carefully selected books can provide sorrow-laden people with valuable understanding as well as encouragement. For example, in *Embracing Life: Growing Through Love and Loss*, psychotherapist Dorothy Corkille Briggs writes this:

> Professionally, I have walked the path with those in deep pain: death, catastrophic illness, divorce, loneliness, confusion, abandonment, and betrayal. Walking with each taught me. Above all I learned that,

reframed, pain does teach if we are open to the lesson.

I remember asking my mother on her seventy-fifth birthday how she felt about reaching that age. Her eyes lit up as she said, "Oh, Dorothy, I've learned more in the past five years than I did in the first seventy!" And this woman had suffered major losses. She knew personally that in spite of devastating losses, each year brought sprouting and newness. Yesterday's disaster is today's teacher if we linger past the pain to learn the lesson.[3]

One of my favorite gift books of all is *The Friendship Factor* by Alan Loy McGinnis. In it this California minister quotes Helen Keller once saying: "With the death of every friend I love, a part of me has been buried. But their contribution to my being of happiness, strength, and understanding remains to sustain me in an altered world."[4]

A book carefully chosen may indeed be a gift that helps heal the hurt of grief. One saying in *Proverbial Philosophy* puts it this way: "A good book is the best of friends, the same today and forever."[5]

When young children are in a family that loses a pet, an excellent book to give them is *When a Pet Dies*, by Fred Rogers, the creator and host of the award-winning television program, "Mr. Rogers' Neighborhood." My grandchildren were three and six when Brando, the family's much-loved nine-year-old Italian Mastiff, died. This large, lovable dog had earned a special place in the hearts of us all. Reading *When a Pet Dies* helped the children understand more about the death of their pet and lifetime companion. It opened up opportunities for discussion about Brando's death and handling the sad feelings it created.

In addition to giving a copy of *When a Pet Dies* to my daughter and son-in-law to read to their children, I photocopied from *Mister*

Rogers Talks With Parents a section on death. Not exactly a "gift" in the usual sense, this information on helping children deal with death not only of pets but also of people was invaluable according to my daughter.

Donating a specially selected book to a library in memory of the deceased can also be a meaningful gesture and tribute. Librarians can help you make an appropriate choice. For years our neighbors admired the beautiful flowers my grandfather grew. They were a great source of pride for him—partly because they gave so much pleasure to others. Then my grandfather died, and about ten days later, my grandmother received a card from the public library indicating that the neighbors had given the library a handsome book on flowering plants, in memory of Granddad. My grandmother was deeply moved.

Memorial Gifts to Charitable Causes

Contributing to a charitable cause or a special interest of the deceased can be a gift that helps heal the hurt. Many families list preferred charities in the obituary. Simply by knowing the deceased person and the family you usually will be aware of their interests. Consider the case of Jerry Jamieson and his fiancée Jill, two of the most attentive and conscientious students in a college course I taught on marriage. Jill had cystic fibrosis but, undeterred, the two were married. They both suspected that Jill would probably live only a few short years. Their dreams were cut even shorter than that. Jill died two months after their wedding. Some of the couple's friends made contributions in Jill's memory to the national cystic fibrosis research program. "This meant a great deal to me," Jerry says. "In some small way, it helped give me hope that something positive and worthwhile might come from Jill's death."

Another meaningful gift was given in memory of Lynda Manning.

Lynda and a friend had both been saying for several years that when they were old enough they were going to work as Candy Stripers at a Ronald McDonald House, a place where parents and siblings of seriously ill children can stay while the children are receiving medical care. After Lynda's death, the parents of Lynda's friend gave a gift of money in memory of Lynda to the Ronald McDonald House in Temple, Texas. Says Lorita, "This gift was comforting because it keeps alive the spirit of Lynda's wanting to help others."

Another gift the Mannings said was especially consoling was a prayer bench some friends gave in memory of Lynda to Latham Springs, a Christian encampment near Waco, Texas. "It is my hope and prayer," says Lorita, "that when someone goes to the prayer garden and sees the inscription, 'In Memory of Lynda Manning, March 7, 1972 – November 16, 1985,' they will prayerfully dedicate their life to God as Lynda did, so that they can enjoy eternity with their heavenly Father, just as Lynda is doing right now."

Friends might also give something very practical—like a needed piece of furniture to a church in memory of a deceased person. Vina, a widow for about three years, tells how a gift of a pew was comforting to her after Bob's death: "We always sat on the same pew at church, and we kiddingly said, 'This is our pew.' Others also said in jest, 'You'd better not sit in Bob and Vina's pew.'"

When Bob died, friends were searching for ways to respond and to minister to Vina. At about that time their church renovation was completed, and there was a need for additional pews. Money was short, so the call went out for donations. Several friends got together and gave enough money to buy one of the larger pews, a beautiful mahogany one. Pews that had been bought in memory of someone had an attractive bronze plaque on the arm of the pew, telling who had been memorialized. Said Vina, "Bob always had such a sense of humor. He would love this—really having a pew with his name on it."

"No Strangers in Our Midst"

Sometimes when tragedy strikes, family and friends are simply not available right away. That is when we can step in and give much-needed gifts—often very practical ones—to complete strangers. For instance, on August 2, 1985, the ill-fated Delta Flight 191 claimed the lives of 133 people on the runway of the Dallas/Fort Worth International Airport. Injured survivors were taken to area hospitals, including Parkland Memorial Hospital (where decades ago national attention focused on efforts to save the life of our President, John Fitzgerald Kennedy).

Over thirteen hundred people waited in lines at that hospital to give a most precious gift—blood—to try to save lives of people they did not even know. Ron J. Anderson, MD, President and Chief Executive Officer of Parkland, commented, "It was simply overwhelming." People offered similar gifts when Catherine O'Shea was far from home and her husband was killed. She said she learned from that experience that "we are all family and that, truly, there are no strangers in our midst."[6]

Other Comforting Gifts

Snapshots

Lorita Manning told me about some other very comforting gifts given to her and her family after Lynda died. Many of Lynda's friends, for example, searched through snapshots they had and pulled together numerous ones that included Lynda. Then they put them in an attractive photo album and gave it to the Mannings.

Scrapbooks

A similar gift was a lovely fabric-covered scrapbook with a framed picture of Lynda on the front of it. A relative who made these albums created an especially attractive one to give to the Mannings for saving cards and notes received after Lynda's death.

Audio recordings

The funeral for Lynda was a commemoration of her short but purposeful life. "The words spoken were well chosen," says Lorita, "and they helped us make some sense out of Lynda's untimely death." A friend recorded the service and gave it to the Mannings. "That gift meant a lot. It took some planning ahead."

If you have a recording of the voice of the deceased, you might consider giving that to loved ones. A friend of mine, for example, had recorded a conversation between himself and an elderly man who had been his friend for years. The friend asked questions about the elderly man's childhood, about his early ranching days, and about his philosophy of life—the man was highly regarded for his civic contributions to the community. After the man died, my friend had copies made and gave one to each of the man's children.

Videos

I heard of a similar gift involving a video. Several different parents had video recorded a school program. Several months afterwards, a young girl who had participated in the program was killed in a car wreck. A friend of the girl's family contacted the teacher, found out who had recorded the program, paid for a duplicate to be made, and gave this to the parents. Cherishing that recording, the parents were comforted by the fact that someone would go to some trouble to get such a prized gift to give to them.

Gravesite maintenance

Another gesture that the Mannings said was a special gift of comfort to them had to do with Lynda's gravesite. "Some friends knew of our plans for the first visit there after the service," explains Lorita, "so they went ahead, trimming the grass . . . making sure everything looked attractive." Lorita continues, "Because of our friends' thoughtfulness, we were able to concentrate on the words we'd had engraved in the pink granite headstone: "This is our beloved daughter, in whom we are well pleased. . . .""

Special music

Another very comforting gift is a willingness to use musical talents for the funeral service. Lorita Manning describes one such memorable gift: "Charlotte Bowling, Lynda's choir director, not only gave her musical expertise, she gave of herself when she so beautifully sang the words of 'I Am a Promise' at Lynda's funeral. It truly was a gift of comfort to us."

Share family heritage

Certain other gifts may need to be given which only you can provide. When Dale left home to go into the service, some of his possessions were stored at his mother and father's. With Dale's permission, a younger brother, Craig, wore one of Dale's rings—a beautiful gold one. Dale in the meantime married, had two children, and then was killed during the Tet

Offensive in the Vietnam War. By word of mouth several years later, Craig heard that Dale's son, Bruce, had mentioned that he longed to know more about his father. Craig, by this time, was married and had a family of his own as well as a demanding job. Nevertheless, Craig knew there was something he must do—something he wanted to do out of appreciation for what Dale meant to him in their years at home together. With his own family's support and with the full agreement of Dale's widow, Craig went across the United States to get Bruce, and the two of them traveled together, tracing some of the favorite vacation routes Dale and Craig had enjoyed with their family years before. Craig also took Bruce to the family farm—by then owned by others, but Craig had contacted them, asking if he and Dale's son could traipse over the old home site. The current owners, of course, agreed.

Craig shared stories with Dale's son that the boy's father never had the chance to relate. He introduced Bruce to several of Dale's former teachers who had been favorites and to Dale's high school football coach. A visit with several of Dale's high school friends was especially rewarding.

Then on the last evening of Craig and Bruce's five-day trip, Craig gave Bruce Dale's gold ring. Bruce says he remembers Craig saying something like this: "Your dad was a great guy. Just as we've traced some of his tracks, he'd want you to make some tracks of your own, some that in a few years you can look back on and feel good about. I just pray to God that when you grow up and if you have a son, you'll get to live to share life together. Whatever happens, I want you to know I'm available . . . and here's a ring your dad liked a lot, but he was generous enough to let me wear it. Now it's yours. Wear it with pride, remembering your dad loved you and dreamed of having a son like you." Bruce says the time his uncle spent with him and the sharing about his dad were invaluable—gifts in the truest sense—and the ring is a gift that still comforts him as it reminds him of those precious memories.

A box of happy thoughts

Yet another type of gift that can uplift is a collection of cheerful thoughts, quotes, or sayings. A friend of mine routinely clips out or makes copies of these as she sees them. Now she has an extensive collection, and when someone dies, she gives a decorated box filled with them to the bereaved person. Her accompanying note may say something like: "My thoughts and prayers are with you, but when you need a boost, just read some of these happy thoughts." The little box will be full of encouraging words like these:

> I believe in the sun
> Even when it is not shining
> I believe in love
> Even when I am alone
> I believe in God
> Even when He is silent.
> * * *
> Tomorrow has two handles:
> the handle of fear and
> the handle of faith.
> You can take hold of it by either handle.
> * * *
> It is better to light candles than to curse the darkness.

In *Triumph Over Tears* a similar gift was described:

> About a month after Galen died, a friend mailed
> me a bright red box. It said EILEEN'S SMILE BOX
> on the outside and was about the size of a cigar box.
> There was a smiling face on the outside. Inside were
> bright squares of construction paper and each had a
> handwritten message.
>
> They were all quick and easy to read, and to the
> point. One I still remember said, "Life, like the Bactrian
> camel, has two humps—one to carry the burdens of
> yesterday, and the other, the hopes of tomorrow." I
> think that quote was by William Walter DeBolt. Some
> were by Norman Vincent Peale.
>
> That was the nicest thing anyone did for me
> when I was first widowed. Anyone could make one of
> those boxes.[7]

The adaptation of both of these ideas is providing a collection of
especially inspiring verses from the Bible. These could be written
on individual pieces of paper, in a small booklet, or perhaps on
a calendar. Example verses from the Bible that might prove
particularly comforting to a bereaved person are the following:

> "Peace I leave with you, my peace I give unto
> you: not as the world giveth, give I unto you. Let not
> your heart be troubled, neither let it be afraid." (John
> 14:27)
>
> "Thou wilt keep him in perfect peace, whose
> mind is stayed on thee." (Isaiah 26:3)
>
> "My presence shall go with thee, and I will give

thee rest." (Exodus 33:14)

"They shall come home and sing songs of joy and shall be radiant over the goodness of the Lord. Their life shall be like a watered garden, and all their sorrow shall be gone." (Jeremiah 31:12, *The Living Bible*)

"Lo, I am with you always, even unto the end of the world." (Matthew 28:30)

"I will never leave thee, nor forsake thee." (Hebrews 13:5)

"Be strong and of good courage, do not fear or be in dread, for it is the Lord your God who goes with you; he will not fail you or forsake you." (Deuteronomy 31:6, *Revised Standard Version*)

Gifts that reflect your personal touch, like these little collections of sayings and poems and verses from the Bible, are generally even more healing than other gifts. Where do you get these? Just about everywhere. Here is one I saw on a bumper sticker: "Nothing can happen to me today that God and I can't handle together." This one I copied from a well-worn magazine in my doctor's office: "You cannot prevent the birds of sorrow from flying over your head, but you can prevent them from building nests in your hair."

An all-time favorite is one that appears frequently here and there. It is said to be an old Irish verse:

> May the road rise up to meet you.
> May the wind be always at your back.
> May the sun shine warm upon your face,
> And the rain fall soft upon your fields,
> And until we meet again,

May God hold you in the palm of His hand.

A church I pass several times a week always displays a positive and thought-provoking saying—a different one each week. This is one I saw a year or so ago, and I have included it in my collection: "Jesus is the Light that never has a power failure."

One of my very favorites came from a friend who is a member of Alcoholics Anonymous. She says this prayer, originally composed by a Massachusetts preacher, is the motto of AA: "God, grant me serenity to accept the things I cannot change, courage to change the things I can, and the wisdom to know the difference."

Travel fare

Lynnette Pontius received one of the most touching—and most appreciated—gifts of all. Lynnette was a student at a Texas university when her twenty-eight-year-old sister, Lisa, died suddenly in Denver. Lisa was about eight months pregnant at the time. Lisa and Lynnette's parents lived in Tulsa, Oklahoma, and they left for Denver immediately. They encouraged Lynnette to stay in Texas, knowing her finances were very tight and feeling there was nothing that she could really do at home or at the service. But a thoughtful gift made possible a very healing good-bye. Here's how Lynnette tells the story:

> Some of my professors and a few members of the university administration heard about Lisa's death, and they bought me a plane ticket so I could go to the funeral. I got to Denver before Lisa's baby died. Getting to touch him before he died was sort of like getting to say

good-bye to Lisa. Going to the funeral was the saddest experience in my life. Yet in many ways it was also the most comforting part of the entire ordeal. I will never forget that gift—the airplane ticket—it's one of the most heartfelt gifts I ever received.

Note cards and stamps

My aunt said one very useful gift she received when my uncle died was a large packet of note cards and a roll of stamps for all the messages that needed to be written after the funeral. Another friend helped address the cards. My aunt commented: "Getting all the addresses seemed like a hurdle I simply couldn't handle. When a friend offered to help me, I felt like she had given me a very precious and practical gift."

Gifts and the Giver

Thinking of a gift that will be personalized and especially comforting is sometimes difficult. On the other hand, some gifts which are healing to the bereaved can be equally gratifying to the giver of the gift. Consider the gift Brett gave to Mrs. Mills, a neighbor who had been like a grandmother throughout his growing up. After Mr. Mills died, fourteen-year-old Brett commented to his father, "I wish I knew something I could do to help Mrs. Mills. She seems so sad." A heavy silence filled the room as both sank deep into thought. "I've got it!" Brett shrieked, shattering the quiet. "Every week when Mom takes Mrs. Mills to the doctor to get her shots, I'll mow her lawn, and she'll never know who did it." Brett was right. Mrs. Mills never knew for sure who mysteriously mowed her lawn every week for the two summers before she died. But Brett knew.

Many other givers of gifts as well as recipients of well-thought-out gifts have shared with me how these gifts can bless the giver as well as the recipient. Their experiences vouch for the validity of this age-old truth: "Give generously, for your gifts will return to you." (Ecclesiastes 1:1, *The Living Bible*)

Here is another variation of this universal truth—in this case a mother's gifts were returned to her daughter in a clever and comforting way. Nan was always collecting and sharing ideas, recipes, poems, and other choice bits of information with friends. Everyone was dismayed when Nan discovered that she had cancer of the pancreas. Nan lived only five months after that diagnosis. Nan's daughter, Carol, had postponed her wedding date because of her mother's terminal illness, but several months after her mother's death she did get married. Carol's new home was decorated in the country motif, and, as she put it, "I want the walls plastered with family pictures and warm and inviting things."

Several of Nan's friends "pooled their resources," so to speak. Imogene had a copy of a cornbread recipe Nan had written out for her. Sara had a copy of this saying which Nan had paraphrased and given to her:

> Happiness is like trying to catch a butterfly.
> If you try to trap it, it will surely fly away.
> If you sort of ignore it while you go about
> doing good for others,
> It'll come sit on your shoulder.

Another friend, Jean, had a copy of a favorite prayer written out in Nan's beautiful handwriting. These friends had these items matted and framed for Carol's new country kitchen. Says Carol, "Mother's friends went to a lot of trouble and gave up things my mother had given them. I cherish these gifts, for they capture the indomitable spirit of my mother."

The Gift of Listening

A gift that can be given over and over again and never lose its usefulness is simply listening. As pointed out in the second chapter, grieving people need someone to talk to, someone who will listen. When we take the time to listen attentively, we offer a gift that will help the hurt of losing a loved one to death. "Listening is a gift you can give, no matter who you are. And you can give it to anyone. It doesn't cost a cent, but it is priceless to a person who needs a listener."[8]

We feel compelled to say something to help our grief-stricken friend when a simple "I'm sorry" and our caring, attentive silence may be the best approach. Our heartbroken friends will feel freer to talk if we do not monopolize the entire conversation. The sixth century Roman monk and Christian theologian, Dionysius, said, "Let your speech be better than silence, or be silent." Another author says: "Helping your friend to open up and talk is one of the greatest gifts you can give. Like lancing a boil, though, it takes directness and sensitivity."[9]

Listening to bereaved friends not only helps them work through their grief, but listening also helps us to know other ways we might help them. As Tacitus, the early Roman historian put it, "To know a person, close your eyes and open your ears." But being a good listener doesn't just mean being silent. Sometimes it means freeing the bereaved to talk by following through with an appropriate question.

Consider this situation, for example. People were gathered around the tables for a Wednesday night dinner at church. Annie Ruth had been a widow for six months. She turned to the person to her left and said, "I've been able to get through some big milestones since my husband's death—like choosing the headstone. But the other day I had a flat tire—the first one since my husband died, and I went to pieces." The person said nothing, perhaps not knowing what to say.

In a few moments Annie Ruth turned to the person on her right and repeated her comments. That person said, "That must've been tough. How did you handle it?" Annie Ruth's pent-up words came tumbling out. "The flat tire itself was not unmanageable," she explained, "but it was simply a painful reminder that my husband had always been there to fix flat tires, and now he wasn't." After Annie Ruth poured out her pain, she added, "I have plenty of friends who've said they'd help if I'd just call, but I'd like to be independent." To that comment the friend replied, "Have you considered joining an automobile service association?" Then the conversation developed around how to explore this possibility. Asking gentle questions and then quietly listening helped heal some of Annie Ruth's hurt. Like most grieving people, listening was truly a gift she needed.

Better Than a Gift

A line in the Apocrypha describes a healing gift my mother gave to a grief-stricken friend: "So is a word better than a gift." Let me explain. Cora's husband had died, and Cora became an even more intense worrier than ever. My mother was an optimistic person with a gift of encouraging others. She had offered solace in various compassionate ways. She had been a good listener, and she had also tried to help Cora realize that chronic worry and fretting were accomplishing nothing. Mother commented, "I tried serious talks as well as kidding ones." She elaborated that she once made this point to Cora: "Worry is like rocking in a rocking chair—it takes some effort and is somewhat satisfying, but it simply doesn't get you anywhere."

"The words that helped Cora the most though," said Mother,

"were ones which shared my own experiences with worry." Two of Mother's sons spent about twenty years each in the military, and a third one spent two years as a paratrooper. All were in the service during the Vietnam War. "I worried—and prayed—a lot for several years," Mother admitted. My sister, Janet, was the only one of my mother's children who had not moved from our hometown. "I worried about the boys in the service," said Mother, "and I worried about the others traveling here and there—especially Barbara traveling and working in Africa." She continued, "Not once did it enter my mind to worry about Janet. We visited with each other frequently in our peaceful New Mexico town. We had shopped and enjoyed a soft drink together that Saturday afternoon only a few hours before she and her husband were hit and killed by a drunk driver just three blocks from their home."

Mother shared her feelings about worry with Cora and said, "Cora, my experience with worry has proven to me the things we worry about rarely happen, and worry would not change the outcome anyway. So why worry?" Cora told me that Mother's telling her this made an impact on her. Words spoken in Job aptly describe this situation: "How forcible are right words!" (Job 6:25) Concludes Cora, "The firm but loving words this dear friend took time to share with me were just what I needed." In Cora's case, words were indeed "better than a gift."

An Unusual Gift

The parents of Blake, a college student who died in an auto collision, describe an unusual gift that was of special comfort to them. Blake and some other students had gone to a ballgame in a city about two hours away from their own campus. On the return trip, about halfway home, there was some confusion about the proper lanes in a construction area. A head-on collision claimed the lives of the drivers of both vehicles at the scene of the accident. Blake and two other passengers were taken to a nearby hospital. A carload of students from Blake's school was following the car Blake was riding in, saw the accident, stopped and helped with emergency treatment, and then followed the ambulances to the hospital. One of the students knew Blake and Blake's roommate, Gregg. He called Gregg, a pre-med student who had stayed home to study for an upcoming exam. Gregg arrived at the hospital within the hour.

The doctors expressed dim hope for Blake. Gregg recalled how on several occasions he and Blake had talked about donating their organs if something should happen to either of them. Gregg struggled in his mind whether or not to tell Blake's parents about their conversations. By the time Blake's parents arrived at the hospital, Gregg was prepared to tell them of Blake's wishes.

Blake lived only forty-eight hours after the crash. During this time, his parents thought over the possibility of donating their only son's organs. They did not know much about how to go about it, and they had some preconceived ideas about it all. They had the mistaken notion, for example, that Blake's body would be disfigured and they would not be able to have a funeral service. They talked to the doctors, who patiently answered their questions. Blake's parents soon knew they wanted to carry out their son's wish.

In Blake's dying, he gave life and sight to others. One kidney went to save the life of a four-year-old boy in another state. One went to a mother who had been driving sixty miles every week to be on a dialysis machine for six hours each day. Blake's donated kidney enabled this mother to resume a more normal life and to be at home with her two school-age children and her husband. Blake's eyes restored sight to a school teacher and to a young man who later completed a degree in counseling and guidance. Other organs were donated to a research program at a medical school.

Blake's parents still feel a strong sense of gratitude to Gregg for having the courage to approach them during those excruciating hours right after the collision. Blake's father says he remembers how Gregg said something like, "This is really hard for me to say, but I feel I must tell you something Blake said earlier this semester. Then the choice is yours." Says Blake's mother, "We were so stunned and paralyzed by Blake's certain death, we never would've thought about donating his organs until it was too late." Blake's mother adds that their decision to donate Blake's organs was the most consoling part of his death. As she put it, "This was sort of a gift of life to others."

A Gift of Faith and Forgiveness

A copy of the Bible turned out to be the most healing gift another college student received after he killed his best friend. Let me explain. Bill and his friend—they had been friends since junior high school days—had been drinking one evening at Bill's apartment when they decided to go for a drive. Bill remembers little of what happened, but witnesses say he was driving at an excessive speed when he swerved off the highway, hitting an embankment. Bill's friend died immediately while Bill was in intensive care for days, hanging onto that fragile thread between life and death.

Bill explained how he was ashamed and embarrassed and felt miserable about what he had done. Here is how he described his feelings: "I felt that I had committed the worst crime possible . . . killing my best friend and under despicable circumstances, drinking and all that. So many nights I'd lie awake in that hospital bed, wishing I could trade my life for his." He continued, "My mom and dad must've been crushed. The story appeared in newspapers all over Nebraska, and people in our Illinois hometown knew about it.

"But they didn't turn their backs on me," said Bill. "Mom and Dad flew to Lincoln to be with me. I was in the hospital there over a month. The love my parents showed helped pull me through. They'd tell me things to help cheer me up. Dad said my friend wouldn't want me to feel guilty or go around the rest of my life feeling sorry for myself or punishing myself. But I guess Dad knew my self-recrimination was so deep that it would require a miracle to get rid of it and not just a few cheerful pep talks. Dad gave me a special copy of the Bible. Oh, I had copies of the Bible before, but I had never read them seriously." Bill continued, "I was desperate though and in deep despair, so I started listening to some of the Scriptures my dad read to me as I was 'tied down' with all those tubes."

Bill paraphrased some of the Scriptures he enjoyed most. He laughingly said, "That story about the prodigal son really hit home." Then Bill said, "This Scripture was the one that I needed more than anything else: 'There is therefore no condemnation for those who are in Christ Jesus.' (Romans 8:1, *Revised Standard Version*) When I realized that God could forgive me for drinking and driving crazy and killing my best friend—and I asked him to do just that—I experienced the peace that I had thought impossible."

Bill elaborated, "I also felt it was very important that I ask my best friend's parents to forgive me. That was the toughest thing I have ever done in my whole life, but it was something I had to do. When they came to the hospital, I was braced for whatever might happen. In fact, I thought they had a right to refuse my invitation to come. Why would they want to have anything to do with me?"

Bill described how terror gripped him when the parents of his dead friend entered his room. "Our eyes locked. I have never felt so guilty, so worthless, so afraid in all my life," said Bill. He described how his friend's mother came over to him, put her hands on his shoulders, and stood quietly with her husband right by her side. "Our son loved you," she said, "and we love you." Then an even more persuasive smile came over her face as she said, "And God loves you!"

The Bible describes forgiveness and healing that is not humanly possible, says Bill today. "I am thankful that my parents gave me that special gift and lived out the forgiveness and love portrayed in the Bible. And my best friend's parents—only God's love could enable them to forgive me for killing their son." Concludes Bill, "The Bible and the kind of forgiveness described in it were the gifts that helped heal my horrible hurt, and this line from the Bible summarizes my gratitude: 'Thanks be unto God, for his unspeakable gift. . . .'" (Second Corinthians 9:15)

A Gift without End

Friends can make the difference when disaster strikes—they can help the soul-torn triumph over it by giving just the right gift. They did just that in the case of the Shepherd family. Six-year-old Sheri Shepherd was very sick. Everyone knew from her appearance her short life would soon end. Sheri had suffered extensive physical and emotional pain during her three-year bout with leukemia, but she complained little and asked for no special favors. However, she admitted to her grandmother, "More than anything I would like to have a Cabbage Patch doll." Medical expenses had drained the family's financial resources. Other expenses had added to the financial burden, such as moving closer to Houston for Sheri's treatment. Sheri's mother had to quit her job because of the move and because of the demands Sheri's illness made on her time. A Cabbage Patch doll was simply out of the question.

Some friends of Sheri's grandmother heard about Sheri's wish. They were all touched by the dying child's desire. But they did not stop there; they rallied around and gathered enough contributions to pay for the doll. However, they were unable to find one. Cabbage Patch dolls were the rage at the time, and stores sold out of them very quickly. Undaunted, the grandmother called several stores known to sell the popular dolls. The manager of one of the stores had two children himself, one the age of Sheri. He told the caller, "I have two robust children. I sometimes take their health for granted. I am going to do what it takes to get you a Cabbage Patch doll for Sheri." With some long distance calls and explanations, a Cabbage Patch doll exactly like Sheri wanted was located. "Sheri and that doll were inseparable," says Sheri's mother, "and I am convinced that doll helped ease Sheri's pain those last awful days."

Sheri's parents say they still are comforted by the very thought of all the people pulling together to provide the doll for Sheri. The story of this gift did not stop with Sheri's death. Because that gift—and the thought behind the gift—meant so much to Sheri and to her parents, upon Sheri's death the parents requested that people wanting to send flowers, food, or other gifts find a terminally ill child instead. "Find out what would bring some joy to that child and ease the burden of the parents," suggested Sheri's father. People have done just that, so this story has no ending. It is being reenacted over and over as other parents make the same request that Sheri's parents did. In this case, giving a gift to a very ill child is truly giving a gift that keeps on giving.

People who successfully survive the death of a loved one, more often than not, have one or more close friends or relatives who help them throughout their tragedy. How do these friends help heal the hurt? What steps do they take to comfort those who grieve? One of the steps is to give a carefully chosen gift that takes into consideration the special needs and circumstances of the hurting ones. The gift may be something tangible such as flowers, or a book, or it may be a special gesture or act of kindness. The main concern is giving or doing something that will show you care. That is the kind of gift that will keep on giving.

Step 7

Extend an Invitation
If you really care...

"When the people have gone home . . ."
"When the cards stop coming . . ."
"When the telephone ceases to ring . . ."
" . . . then the hardest time begins."

These are words I have heard repeatedly from grief-stricken individuals following the death of someone close to them or after some other tragic loss. Those genuinely wanting to help others handle their grief would do well to remember that recovering from heartbreak is not limited to the first few months. Some very difficult times often occur even months later when everyone else seems to have forgotten about the death or other crisis. Here is what one bereaved person had to say:

I was surprised at the people who tried to comfort me the first few months. Friends and neighbors brought food. People called I hadn't heard from in years. It helped to know people cared. People were compassionate at first, and I am grateful—but about the time the shock of the death wore off and the grim reality hurled me into deeper despair, everybody else was "back to business as usual."

Another recovering griever expresses the feelings of many who have suffered a painful loss: "If you really care, you'll reach out, and continue to reach out."

Ways to Reach Out

Extending an invitation is one way to reach out, for invitations can help fill that awful emptiness a death or other loss creates. Invitations can be quite simple, says Dr. Paul Stripling, clergyman, interim executive director of a large association of churches in Central Texas, and noted grief counselor. "Simply consider what the bereaved person liked to do before the death. Chances are, the person probably would still enjoy those same things. For example, did he or she like to eat out? Go to plays? Take walks or drives?" Dr. Stripling suggests even a brief call to invite the bereaved to join you on some errands would be a thoughtful gesture. June, a friend of mine, says that the first few months after her husband's funeral, even a simple trip to the supermarket was difficult. "Now I always ask a new widow to let me accompany her to the grocery store," she says. In the case of my newly widowed mother-in-law, an invitation from a friend to share a pew at church on Sunday morning did wonders for her.

Invite Yourself Over

Ava Trudeau remembers an invitation that was particularly helpful to her after the crushing death of her husband, Jeff. "Facing life after Jeff died," says Ava, "was very hard." Jeff died unexpectedly from a massive heart attack. Ava recounts how inconsolable she felt after her children and other relatives had gone home. One evening she plunked down onto the sofa, hit by a wave of self-pity. "Why me, God?" Ava asked, struggling to make some sense out of it all. "At least Jeff died quickly and with little pain," Ava recalls saying aloud as she remembered the lingering disease that had taken her brother's life. Ava was grasping at straws to console herself when the doorbell rang.

Startled, she went to the door. When she opened it, she was even more stunned. There stood eight people—Jeff's brother and his wife, who lived an hour's drive away; a couple who lived somewhere in the neighborhood (Ava didn't know where); a couple Jeff and Ava had spoken to on their evening walks; and a young woman with her seven-year-old son who had occasionally joined Jeff and Ava for a short stint on their walks (coincidentally, the friendly boy's name was also Jeff). Finally someone announced, "We've invited ourselves over." Added another voice, "for a potluck supper."

Only then did Ava realize they each indeed did hold in their hands a pan, dish, or a carryout box of something that smelled appetizing. Ava's shock then turned into a flood of tears she had been fighting back. However, the tears soon changed into gentle laughter, Ava relates. "We talked and ate, and then talked some more," says Ava. "Then my brother-in-law and his wife went home. So did one of the other couples." After that, according to Ava, the one remaining man said to his wife, to Ava, and to the young woman and her son, "Now I guess it's time for our walk."

"This thoughtful gesture of faithful relatives and new-found friends was a major milestone in battling my grief and facing life without Jeff," admits Ava. "Now when one of my friends or relatives loses a loved one," says Ava, "at a time and in the way that seems best, I just invite myself over."

Difficult? Yes. However, inviting ourselves over and extending considerate invitations to the bereaved may also be among the most meaningful ways to help heal the hurt of their loss. Thousands of voices echoing from the past have said so. Kahlil Gibran, an early twentieth-century philosopher and essayist, put it this way: "You give but little when you give of your possessions; it is when you give of yourself that you truly give."

A Special Day

Consider the case of Kim Parker. Kim's mother died the summer Kim turned seventeen. "It was two weeks before my birthday," recalls the Temple, Texas, woman, now an adult. "And toward the end of every summer, Mom and I always combined my birthday with a full day of shopping for school clothes in Dallas. It was our special day together." Kim's friend, Cari, knew this. "So several days before that first birthday after my mother died," Kim says, "Cari called me and asked me if I would like to come with her and her mother shopping for school clothes." On the surface, she notes, that may not sound like much. "But for me, at that age, this was probably the most thoughtful thing anyone did for me after Mom died."

Everyday Activities

The suffering of children, including teenagers like Kim who have lost a parent or some other close relative, is almost incalculable. Yet, too often, grieving children suppress their emotions and get lost in the shuffle when grown-ups are busy consoling grown-ups. This stifling of grief, says a report by the National Academy of Science, can continue "for many years" unless someone steps in to help the child. Meaningful invitations can help. In her book, *How It Feels When a Parent Dies*, Jill Krementz quotes the experiences of eighteen children and how caring people helped them handle their grief after their mother or father died. Comments nine-year-old Alletta Laird made after her father died, for instance, provide insight into how a grieving child feels:

> At our school they told my class that my father had died, and it sort of made me mad because nobody ever played with me. I guess they were embarrassed. It's hard because they think you're different. I've never known anyone else whose father died. But if I did, I would try to cheer her up. I'd invite her over a lot. It would help if your friends could just play with you and treat you like you're a normal person.[1]

Another example involves Gail Gugle, who was seven years old, and her younger brother, Greg. After their father was killed in a car accident, the kind man who lived next door helped them. Gail calls him "Uncle Mike." He's a "pretend uncle," Gail says, "sort of like a father to us now that Daddy's gone."[2] Gail explained how their neighbor invited her and Greg to go jogging with him. He also invited them to bring their bikes to him to fix whenever they were broken. In addition, he invited Greg to play on a soccer team he was coaching. These invitations were quite simple. Yet they provided invaluable comfort and encouragement for two young fatherless children.

Fourteen-year-old Helen Colón lost her mother to multiple sclerosis. Her adjustment problems were complicated by the absence of her father, who lives in Puerto Rico. But invitations by a "big sister" made all the difference. "The person who's been closest to me since my mother's death," Helen says, "is a woman named Mary Woodell, who is like my big sister. There is an organization called Big Brothers, which has many men and women who want to be friends with kids who have lost a parent through death or divorce. I learned about it from a guidance counselor. He said, 'You should call up this place so you'll have someone to pal around with.' My mother died in September, and I got my new big sister in October."

Helen feels that they were matched or paired because Mary's mother also died when she was very young. "We see each other every weekend," Helen says. Mary invites Helen to go with her to the movies and ice-skating. Helen adds, "We just got into roller-skating this year. We also go out to eat a lot. That's something that we both love to do."[3]

Another example of how children are frequently ignored rather than given meaningful invitations to share in the grief process when an adult dies "hits closer to home" for me. My father was married before he married my mother. His first wife died in pregnancy-related complications when both of their sons, Bob and Bill, were too young to even remember their mother. After their father married my mother and had three children (two sons and a daughter—me), he was tragically killed. Bob was eight years old at that time. Now a great-grandfather himself, he remembers that no one told him that his father had been killed. Of course, with all the commotion and adult tears, he realized that something terrible had happened.

Moreover, no one discussed with Bob what was going to happen to him and Bill. No one asked him to talk about his feelings. While the adults in the extended family were doing all the talking and crying, Bob and his younger brother, Bill, were virtually ignored and whisked away to different grandparents. They did not even have each other to talk and cling to. The grandparents were so consumed by their own grief that they did not take their grandsons to visit their step-mother (my mother), who loved them dearly but was engulfed in her own grief and taken to be with her parents, who helped with her three very young children.

This painful personal example happened decades ago. Although the scars of grief were deep, Bob overcame them—he earned BS and MS degrees in engineering from Purdue University, had a stellar career as an officer in the Navy, and now enjoys retirement with his wife of 50-plus years and four children, grandchildren, and a great-grandchild. In addition, he and I get together at least once a year to celebrate our mutual birthday. Unfortunately, no such invitations were extended in our childhood; we only "re-connected" as adults. Nowadays people would, hopefully, be more aware of the importance of including children in the grief process—but I have observed that, unfortunately, they often are not.

This true story from my own family as well as these other true stories illustrate people of all ages, young or old, can extend comforting invitations to people of all ages. In addition, encouraging invitations may be extended to bereft people you know well, to a saddened child your child knows, to mournful members of your neighborhood, and to grief-stricken individuals you meet through community organizations. Equally important to know, invitations can be extended to merely everyday activities. You do not have to wait for a special occasion to offer companionship and encouragement to those who grieve.

The First Year

Invitations throughout the first year after a death can be helpful. The first birthday, the first wedding anniversary, holidays, the first major events—these all can be striking reminders that the loved one is dead and often rekindle burning grief. The first death anniversary may be especially painful. Loved ones might also experience anticipatory grief in the days leading up to significant anniversaries: here again, well-timed, considerate invitations can soften the pangs of grief. For example, Jim and Karen remembered the birthday of Mary Lynn, their good friends' daughter who had been killed in a car wreck. Jim and Karen called several days ahead of the day that would have been Mary Lynn's seventeenth birthday and invited Mary Lynn's parents over for dinner. Mary Lynn's father commented, "To remember the date that would've been our daughter's birthday and to invite us over for dinner was a very thoughtful gesture. It was comforting to be asked to spend that painful evening with friends who cared about us and understood what we were going through."

In my own family, Labor Day weekend was a particularly stressful time for my mother and stepfather because that is when my sister, Janet, and her husband died in a collision caused by a drunk driver. Therefore, everyone made special effort each year to fill this weekend with pleasant visiting.

Other Milestones

Other milestones can also remind people of the death of their loved one. A university chaplain tells about a freshman who was having some tough times during her first semester in college. The student told the university chaplain that she thought she had adjusted to the death of both parents in a train wreck five years ago. "But beginning college is so special," the student explained, "and my parents would enjoy being a part of all this." She added, "This makes me miss them so much."

When the student told the chaplain that she had come from a large, warm Catholic family, he was reminded of his neighbors who fit that same description: "a large, warm Catholic family." Upon hearing about this student's situation, the mother of this family unhesitantly offered invitations that helped ease the girl's grief. Invitations were varied: invitations to join family Sunday get-togethers; to ride to out-of-town football games; to eat holiday meals; to join casual mid-week evening meals; to bring a friend over for a hamburger cookout. These invitations required little extra effort from the parents, but they brought immeasurable comfort and encouragement to a lonely freshman.

Helpful Insights

Betty Jane Wylie offers some helpful insight on invitations in *The Survival Guide for Widows*:

> If you are going to a meeting or a dinner or something that you know the widow will be going to as well, ask her if she wants a lift. Sometimes she gets stubborn (I did) and proud and won't ask for help. But she hopes someone else will think of it. I went to my daughter's high school graduation exercise alone, because I would not ask to go with anyone, and no one thought of asking me to go with them.[4]

Forethought

Charles and Lorita Manning were invited to attend what would have been their daughter Lynda's graduation from junior high school. In addition, Charles was asked to give the address. He worked in the administration of the school district, so this was an especially meaningful invitation extended by the school officials. Lynda was granted her diploma posthumously, and her parents were invited to accept it. All these invitations took forethought on the part of some concerned and caring school officials, but as Lorita put it, "Those invitations were very comforting."

Being with Lynda's friends, the parents of Lynda's friends, and Lynda's teachers in one way was a painful reminder to the Mannings of Lynda's conspicuous absence from the graduation ceremonies. On the other hand, being with those who knew Lynda and who cared for her provided solace, say Lynda's parents. That touching experience reinforced their faith in the beautiful and profound message in "The Plan of the Master Weaver" (author unknown), which Charles shared in his presentation that evening:

> My life is but a weaving between the Lord and me.
> I may not choose the colors. He knows what they should be:
> For He can view the pattern upon the upper side
> while I can see it only on this, the underside.
> Sometimes He weaves in sorrow which seems so strange to me;
> but I will trust His judgment, and work on faithfully,
> 'tis He who fills the shuttle, and He knows what is best.
> So I shall weave in earnest, leaving to Him the rest.
> Not till the loom is silent and the shuttles cease to fly
> shall God unroll the canvas and explain the reason why—
> the dark threads are as needed in the Weaver's skillful hand,
> as the threads of gold and silver in the pattern He has planned.

Limitations

Sometimes a person who has lost a loved one may not be able to accept just any invitation. Consider, for example, the elderly who are limited because of illness or frailty. You may simply need to go where they are. The gratitude generally makes the extra effort worth it all. Just by being there, you invite them to think on things other than their own grief. Consider this vignette:

> I knew a woman, a widow, who was trapped by arthritis in a room where she was brought three not-always-inspired meals a day. People who visited her came away with a lift, and so they went back again. She listened to them; she didn't complain about her own aches and pains, which were myriad and severe. She remembered their children's names, and their husbands', and asked about them. She was glad to see them when they came and never referred to how long it had been since she saw them last, if indeed it was a long time. She appreciated whatever was done for her and made her visitor and benefactor feel like a queen for being so gracious, kind, and generous. She made it very easy for people to love her. They wanted to see her again, so they did. That woman was my mother.[5]

Involvement

As this account suggests, helping encourage someone else generally boosts our own spirits. Brad, for example, was devastated when his younger sister died. He missed her, for, as he put it, "We were more than brother and sister—we were good friends." Brad admits now that he also felt guilty. He was adopted, and he thought that if anyone had to die, it should have been him and not his sister. When Brad started working at a local psychiatric center and helping an eleven-year-old schizophrenic boy whose parents had been killed in a plane crash, his own guilt and grief began dissipating. What had happened is capsulized in these lines I copied long ago from a plaque in a hospital gift shop: "You cannot cure your sorrow by nursing it, but you can cure it by nursing another's sorrow." Brad says now, "I am really glad I was invited to help someone else."

Opportunities to Talk

Inviting sorrow-stricken friends out to eat or to other activities they might enjoy also provides opportunities to talk. Although we learned in the second chapter the importance of "listening more and talking less," when we extend an invitation of this nature, we need to keep in mind that our grieving friends may need others to share conversation about the deceased person.

As pointed out earlier, many people avoid talking about the dead loved one and even change the subject if the grief-stricken brings up the name of the deceased. This is not doing your friend a favor. A sensitive, caring friend will talk—and listen—about the deceased if that is what the bereaved wants. First, however, you may need to extend an invitation that gives the bereaved a comfortable opportunity to express himself or herself.

Reassurance

As another healing benefit, when we extend invitations, we allow the bereaved to resume their social life in a more comfortable, natural way. People sometimes avoid asking their grieving friends to go somewhere or do something, thinking their friends will give clues as to when they are ready to interact or participate more socially. This is unfortunate, for grief-stricken persons are more likely to simply stay at home rather than take the initiative. This was true in Kirk's case. Kirk's wife died after a brief illness. All he really felt like doing was staying home and sitting in front of the television for hours on end, which, incidentally, was completely out of character for him.

"I was usually reluctant when someone called to ask me to go out to eat, or something like that," says Kirk. "But I was glad they kept calling, or I would've never gone out again." He continues, "For one thing, I felt guilty for merely wishing I could enjoy myself . . . and I was afraid of what other people would think about my relaxing and laughing. I didn't want to be disrespectful or disloyal to the memory of my wife." Another grieving person said something similar: "I hated my sorrow and yet felt guilty when I forgot about it."[6]

People who have lost loved ones need reassurance from others that it is okay to enjoy life once again and to begin reinvesting themselves in life and other relationships. Offering considerate invitations is one of the most effective ways to offer that reassurance.

Extending invitations to couples who have lost a child may prove especially invaluable. One bereaved parent commented that one of the more difficult things for someone who has not lost a child to understand is the strange divisiveness that may take over a marriage when the parents are bereaved. After all, an outsider would reason, "The two have been through the mill together. They have so much in common. They have shared all that sorrow. They probably never even argue after having undergone such a catastrophe."[7]

This bereaved parent continues, "That is how it looks on the surface, but it just does not always work that way. Yes, they have shared tragedy, disaster, and grief, but these emotions do not necessarily create a tighter bond. Very often, instead of holding them together, the bond becomes so taut it snaps."[8] Statistics, in fact, indicate that the divorce rate jumps for couples who have had a child to die. Perhaps there is an element of blame. Research suggests blame (perceived or actual) is definitely a factor when parents lose a child to Sudden Infant Death Syndrome (crib death). Perhaps the two marriage partners feel it is simply less painful to flee from the anguish than to stay together and try to resolve the grief together. Studies have shown, however, that couples who lose a child to death but who also have a close circle of friends seem to survive the loss with fewer emotional scars than disconsolate couples who do not have many close friends. Expressing love—concern and caring—to couples whose child dies becomes even more important in light of these findings.

Written Commitments and Calendars

Invitations extended to Evelyn, a new widow, were hard to resist. One friend had given her a calendar. The calendar had lovely pictures of flowers on it, which she liked, but the way in which friends used the calendar was what made invitations so appealing. When a performance at the community playhouse theater was coming soon, or a presentation at the nearby university was announced, or when a special event at church was scheduled, one friend or another would call Evelyn and say something like, "Put this date on your calendar . . . it's something you'll enjoy, and we'll pick you up." Having written the commitment on the calendar gave Evelyn something to look forward to, and, of course, it was not quite so easy to avoid making plans when her friends offered the invitation in this way. Evelyn shared with me this thought that offers insight into how her friends helped heal her hurt:

Don't walk in front of me,
I may not follow.
Don't walk behind me,
I may not lead.
Walk beside me and just
be my friend.

Invitations to Self-Help Groups

An invitation that helped Richard McCleery was extended by a friend who asked Richard to meet with a self-help group. For more than three decades Richard had withstood the pressures of a competitive banking career. Nevertheless, as he put it, "My emotional moorings were ripped from me when Sara, my wife for thirty-three years, was diagnosed as being terminally ill and died only six weeks later—on Christmas Eve." A close friend knew that Richard was still struggling with his grief several months after Sara's death. "This friend was genuinely concerned about me. He invited me to a self-help group of people who'd lost a loved one. When I was hesitant, commenting to him that I just wasn't 'into those group things,' he explained how they are simply people, who have lost loved ones, getting together to discuss ways of coping with their loss."

Self-help groups are usually led by a professionally-trained grief counselor assisted by individuals who have experienced the death of a loved one. The leader and the individuals in the group know and understand what the other grief-stricken persons have been through, the feelings with which they are struggling, and some of the practical concerns they are facing. People in self-help groups can be comforting and encouraging to each other, because, as Richard put it, they can honestly say to each other, "I know how you feel."

The self-help group Richard went to was indeed helpful, he now admits. "Several men and women whose marriage partners had died helped lead the group and they provided living proof that you can suffer a terrible loss and yet go on living." Richard explained how these men and women shared ways of coping that had worked for them. For instance, he says, "We all wrote a letter to our dead marriage partner, telling them good-bye and expressing any other unspoken thoughts we needed to say." Richard says that learning to say good-bye and to let go—so that he could start looking to the future—was one of the most valuable things he gained by going to the self-help group. "I'm glad a friend cared enough about me to invite me . . . . He helped show me that there is a future."

Self-help groups generally include people who have experienced a similar loss, such as a spouse or a child, or they have lost a loved one from a specific cause, such as cancer or suicide or murder. Appendix B lists some of these organizations. For local chapters, or for other groups, you can inquire of clergy in your community, look in the classified section of your telephone book, or phone the chaplain's office of a nearby hospital. Your finding out as much information as possible, helping your bereaved friends make a decision about the most appropriate group to attend, and then offering to accompany them to their first meeting seems to be the most effective approach, according to Richard as well as to hosts of others who have benefited from self-help groups.

Invitations for Professional Counseling

Jean, another grief-stricken person, says being invited to a self-help group helped her overcome the despair she felt after her husband, Dave, died. It also led her to seek professional counseling. "I was still sorrow-worn from my mother's death when my husband developed a rare disease—only one person in thousands has it. Dave always thought he was lucky. He came through some terrifying narrow escapes in the war completely unscathed. He used to jokingly say, 'I am a fugitive from the law of averages.'"

After David died, says Jean, "and I began going to this self-help group, I realized I had more deep-seated feelings—more unresolved grief—to deal with than I thought." She went on to explain that years earlier she had had a therapeutic abortion, saying, "I had carried around the heavy guilt about the abortion long enough." Jean recalls how she discussed this with the group leader, who told her about an excellent Christian psychologist. "I immediately made an appointment, before I lost my nerve," she admits. She adds, "The only regret I have is that I didn't know enough about it all to seek out a good counselor years before, and I didn't have a friend who cared enough to be candid and tell me I needed professional help."

Jean elaborates that she feels her experience has made her more sensitive to other people and their problems. "When I sense a friend is struggling," says Jean, "I share out of my own life. I do all I know to do to help my friends who've lost a loved one, but when the timing is right, I always invite them to consider getting professional grief counseling."

Simple But Helpful

Invitations sometimes can be quite simple and still very helpful, according to my mother. "After your father was killed," she told me, "on one hand, I wanted to gather all you children close to me—like a mother hen protects her chicks under her wings. But sometimes," she continued, "I needed time by myself to wrestle with my grief—or to get away from it all." She explained how the offer of friends or relatives to baby-sit, even for a short period, was a sanity-saving invitation. "Other more extensive invitations were also helpful," she added, "like the relatives who asked one or the other of you to spend a weekend, or the friends who asked you to accompany them and their children to some special event, or the time your aunt and uncle took you with them and their daughter to California one summer."

In addition to the important point my mother was making about the helpfulness of extending invitations to the child or children of one-parent families, she made another good point: it is never too late to help someone whose loved one has died. I was nine years old when relatives included me in their California vacation—my father had been dead over eight years. Nonetheless, it was an invitation of tremendous encouragement, Mother said, one that lightened the overwhelming responsibility of rearing children alone.

Take the Initiative

Praise coupled with an invitation helped heal some of Ruth's hurt after her husband died. Ruth had always enjoyed singing, but she had never sung in the church choir. Several weeks after Don died, an acquaintance turned to Ruth after the church service and said, "You have a beautiful voice—you belong in the choir." Ruth literally glowed. Losing her husband had made Ruth feel as though she had nothing left, and this compliment gave her something to hold onto. No doubt, she felt like Mark Twain must have been feeling when he said, "I can live two months on one good compliment."

The compliment did not end there, however. The acquaintance told the choir director about Ruth's good voice and about Ruth's circumstances. The choir director, realizing that Ruth would probably not take the initiative to join the choir—bereaved persons are rarely able to reach out like that—called Ruth on the phone, chatted with her, made her feel like he valued her as a person, and then he invited her to come to the next choir practice. "Come and try out with us. No obligation on your part," he jovially told her. Then the choir director called several women about Ruth's age and told them about Ruth. The one who lived closest to Ruth then promptly called and offered to come by and give Ruth a ride. All this took place about four years ago. Today Ruth's beautiful soprano voice is an almost-indispensable part of the choir. Says Ruth, "All the people who played a part in this will never know how much it helped me after Don died." This true account reminds me of an ageless truth I once read in a marvelous story in the *Reader's Digest*: "Praise is a potent force, a candle in a dark room. It is magic, and I marvel that it always works."[9]

Invite the Grief-Stricken to Church

An invitation to go to church may also help heal the hurt. However, people should take care to avoid inviting the grief-stricken into a situation that might be more hurtful. Just as in the case of Ruth, friends need to consider the situation in order to extend an appropriate invitation. When bereaved persons do not normally attend church, often people hesitate to ask them to their church. As one person put it, "I didn't want to appear pious or self-righteous and embarrass my friend."

If we think of the church as a "shelter for storm victims," as Charles Swindoll speaks of in *Dropping Your Guard*, then we should be able to embrace the non-churchgoing bereaved with understanding and give them time to heal without quoting verses and sounding "churchy." In other words, as Charles Swindoll maintains:

> Churches need to be less like untouched cathedrals and more like well-used hospitals. Places to bleed rather than monuments to look at. Places where you can take your mask off. Places where you can have your wounds dressed.[10]

When the Bereaved Become Frozen in Their Grief

If a person goes on grieving intensely for a year or so, a concerned friend may need to find specific ways to help the grief-stricken cope more positively—possibly some invitations that help them concentrate on the future. First, perhaps we need to consider why people may not be "getting over" their grief. A person who was seventeen when her twenty-year-old brother died gives us a window to her inner feelings:

> We also may feel "special" while grieving. The world seems to stop for us. People wait on us or try to fill many of our everyday needs that no one ever seemed to notice before. Demands on us lessen or cease. We get phone calls, visits, gifts, and letters. Sometimes new people reach out to us. We feel important and cared about. This special treatment is supportive. It may be the only thing that bolsters us as we face the pain of our grief.[11]

Another bereaved person provides additional understanding. Here is what a man whose wife had been dead for five months had to say about this matter:

> Few people call me now. I'm very lonely. No one worries about my meals or how I am managing my time. People suddenly disappeared, assuming I'm fully recovered from my loss. I'm not recovered. My loneliness now seems even worse. I'm embarrassed that I miss feeling special.[12]

Obviously, this is a very sensitive area. Grief-stricken individuals do need friends who accept them and allow them to share their hurts. They need friends who will reach out and try to help them handle their grief. In spite of the best efforts of friends, in a few rare cases people may stay frozen in their grief. Janice admits that she remained immobilized by grief two years after a car wreck took the lives of her husband and son. One of her dearest friends who had, as Janice put it, "stuck with me through thick and thin," one day reminded Janice of the story in the fifth chapter of John of the man who had lain by the pool for thirty-eight years. Jesus confronted him, "Do you want to get well?" (John 5:6, *Modern Language Bible*) Janice's friend asked her, simply, "Do you want to get over this?"

Janice says the question stunned her at first, and then it made her angry. Janice says she told her friend, "You don't understand what it's like to lose your husband and only child!" Janice's friend replied something like this, "No, I don't understand that, but I do understand how you have suffered, and I love you and want you to somehow survive your awful loss. I want you to be able to enjoy living again. I want to see you smile again." Janice smiles now and says, "My friend was very perceptive. She helped me realize that grieving constructively is hard work. She reminded me that Thomas Edison was probably not speaking of grief when he said, 'There's no substitute for hard work,' but the saying sure applies to grief."

Janice's friend helped her make the conscious decision to live again. Says Janice, "My friend reminded me of this beautiful invitation: "Look, today I have set before you life and death. Oh, that you would choose life." (Deuteronomy 30:15, 19, *The Living Bible*)

Janice may never have heard of the late great Harvard psychologist, William James. Nevertheless, she demonstrated one of his observations that I think applies directly to grief work:

"Nothing is as fatiguing as the eternal hanging on of an uncompleted task."[13]

Harmful Invitations

Todd had suffered a loss similar to Janice's—his wife died soon after giving birth to their first child, and the baby died a day later. "Life can change so quickly," he said. "One day we were laughing and looking forward to the birth of our first baby—the next day Joan was dead. Then the following evening our little son died, and I felt dead myself." Says Todd nearly ten years after this double loss, "Friends who were brave enough to stay with me through all the crying and yelling and despondency made all the difference."

Several couples went to the hospital as soon as they learned that Joan had gone into labor. When it became apparent that problems were developing with the delivery, they called other friends and invited them to come to the hospital to join a tight-knit support group for Todd. Some out of this group took turns staying with Todd during the next life-changing thirty-six hours in which both his wife and son died. Since Todd refused to go home to rest during this time, one of the couples invited him to rest at their home, which was near the hospital. Todd says this gesture as well as other seemingly small ones was of tremendous comfort. He remembers how people invited him to eat with them at the hospital cafeteria. Others invited him to eat at their home the evening after Joan died when the baby was still alive but extremely critical. Another couple invited him to ride home with them to spend the night "after it was all over," as Todd put it, while another friend drove Todd's car home.

"Helpful invitations," Todd adds, "didn't end after the funeral. Friends continued to ask me to eat with them, and one family invited me over a lot to use their pool—they knew how much I liked to swim.

Another guy I worked with but didn't even know very well at the time started inviting me to eat lunch with him and some people from his department. A neighbor asked me to join his weekly Toastmasters group." Adds Todd, "All these invitations showed me that my friends really cared about me."

In contrast, Todd admits now there were some invitations he wished some of his friends had not extended—that is, to alcoholic beverages to forget his sorrow. "Friends were well-meaning, but I can see now," Todd explains, "that liquor and even tranquilizers are like putting Band-Aids on gaping wounds. They simply do no good. They may blot out the agony momentarily, but it's still there."

When Bereaved Persons Decline Invitations

People who want to extend appropriate and encouraging invitations to sorrowful friends need to know that bereaved persons frequently decline invitations—or accept only to cancel at the last minute. Dr. Paul Stripling emphasizes that friends who genuinely want to help need patience and understanding. Well known for his knowledge and counseling skills, this grief expert points out, "People in deep mourning may fear losing control of their emotions in front of others. They need to know if their tears do come, they will not bother their friends. Acceptance and gentle encouragement will give them courage to resume life."

Thoughtful invitations, elaborates Dr. Stripling, "will give them something to look forward to and will help them in concrete ways to begin reinvesting themselves in living and to know it is okay to begin enjoying life again." In short, Dr. Stripling says that invitations can provide hope as emphasized in the *Revised Standard Version* of the Bible, Proverbs 23:18: "Surely you have a wonderful future ahead of you. There is hope for you yet!"

Conclusion

❧

My heartfelt gratitude goes out to the hundreds of people who shared with me their experiences of loss and grief. Many emphasized how their personal encounters with death and other losses made them wonder at times if they would ever see the other side of grief. But their experiences also taught them the profound wisdom in this Scripture, "Blessed are those who mourn, for they shall be comforted." (Matthew 5:4, *Revised Standard Version*) "People reaching out in concern and kindness bring special meaning to this Scripture," says one recovering mourner. "An additional thing I have learned," says another, "is how people who help bereaved friends and relatives receive compassionate attention when they in turn lose a loved one or suffer a great hurt." This observation reflects another ageless truth: "Blessed are the merciful, for they shall obtain mercy." (Matthew 5:7, *Revised Standard Version*)

The death of a loved one is devastating as are many other losses. But sincere expressions of caring can help heal horrible hurts. By carrying out one or more of the steps in *Seven Steps for Dealing with Grief,* you can help turn the grief of futility and despair into grief filled with faith and hope. When you really care, you will take steps to live out the wisdom expressed in these lines:

> I am only one,
> But I am one.
> I cannot do everything,
> But I can do something.
> And what I can do
> I ought to do,
> And by the grace of God
> I will do.

St. Francis Prayer for Healers

Lord,
Make me an instrument of your health:
where there is sickness, let me bring cure;
where there is injury, aid;
where there is suffering, ease;
where there is sadness, comfort;
where there is despair, hope;
where there is death, acceptance and peace.

Grant that I may not:
So much seek to be justified, as to console;
to be obeyed, as to understand;
to be honored, as to love . . .
for it is in giving ourselves that we heal,
it is in listening, that we comfort,
and in dying, that we are born to eternal life.

$Notes$

$Step\ 1:\ Be\ There$

1. Elisabeth Kübler-Ross, *On Death and Dying* (New York: Macmillan Publishing Co., 1969), 246.
2. Lily Pincus, *Death and the Family: The Importance of Mourning* (New York: Vintage Books, 1974), 253.
3. N. J. Amar, MD, Interview, April 6, 2008.
4. James J. Lynch, *The Broken Heart* (New York: Basic Books, Inc., Publishers, 1979), 102.
5. Joshua Loth Liebman, *Peace of Mind* (New York: Simon and Schuster, 1946), 113.
6. Lynn Caine, *Widow* (New York: William Morrow and Co., Inc., 1974), 31.
7. Wayne E. Oates, *Anxiety in Christian Experience* (Philadelphia: The Westminster Press, 1955), 52–53.
8. Erich Lindemann, "Grief Management," Speech at the Symposium on Death, Grief, and Bereavement, University of Minnesota, May 18, 1967.
9. Judy Tatelbaum, *The Courage to Grieve* (New York: Harper and Row, Publishers, 1980), 7.
10. John DeFrain, Leona Martens, Jan Stork and Warren Stork, *Stillborn: The Invisible Death* (Lexington, MA: Lexington Books, 1986), 109–110.
11. Ibid., 116.
12. Ibid.
13. Reprinted from *Men: A Book for Women*, (p. 165) by James Wagenvoord. Copyright 1978 by James Wagenvoord. Reprinted by permission of Avon Books.
14. S. I. McMillen, *None of These Diseases* (Old Tappan, NJ: Fleming H. Revell Co., 1963), Preface.

15. From Eda LeShan as quoted in *The Courage to Grieve*, Judy Tatelbaum (New York: Harper and Row, Publishers, 1980), 61.

16. United States Census Bureau. Washington, D.C.

17. Doug Manning, *Don't Take My Grief Away: What to Do When You Lose a Loved One* (San Francisco: Harper and Row, Publishers, 1979), 52.

18. Ibid., 52.

19. Betsy Burnham, *When Your Friend Is Dying* (Grand Rapids, MI: Chosen Books, 1982), 20.

20. DeFrain, *Stillborn: The Invisible Death*, 108.

21. Ibid., 108.

22. Ibid., 109.

23. Ibid., 108.

24. Ibid., 112.

25. Ibid., 108.

26. Tatelbaum, *The Courage to Grieve*, 12.

27. Kübler-Ross, *On Death and Dying*, 34–121.

28. Colin M. Parkes, *Bereavement: Studies of Grief in Adult Life* (New York: International Universities Press, 1972), 39–44; 63–64; 78–83; 86–87; 94; 131; 150–151.

29. Tatelbaum, *The Courage to Grieve*, 7.

30. Manning, *Don't Take My Grief Away*, 49–50.

31. Elisabeth Kübler-Ross, *On Children and Death* (New York: Macmillan Publishing Co., 1983), 146–147.

32. DeFrain, *Stillborn: The Invisible Death*, 87.

33. Tatelbaum, *The Courage to Grieve*, 30.

34. Robert Veninga, *A Gift of Hope* (Boston: Little, Brown and Co., 1985), back cover.

35. DeFrain, *Stillborn: The Invisible Death*, 111.

36. C. S. Lewis, *Surprised by Joy* (New York: Harcourt Brace Jovanovich, Inc., 1956), 21.

Step 2: Talk Less, Listen More

1. Doug Manning, *Comforting Those Who Grieve* (San Francisco: Harper and Row Publishers, 1985), 71.

2. Robert L. Montgomery, *Listening Made Easy* (New York: American Management Association, 1981), 133.

3. Christopher News Notes, No. 195.

4. Manning, *Comforting Those Who Grieve*, 70.
5. Donna and Rodger Ewy, *Death of a Dream* (New York: E.P. Dutton, Inc., 1984), 120.
6. Wilson Mizner, as quoted in Robert L. Montgomery, *Listening Made Easy* (New York: American Management Association, 1981), 65.
7. "One Day at a Time," written by Marijohn Wilkin and Kris Kristofferson. © 1973, Buckhorn Music Publishers, Inc. P. O. Box 120547. Nashville, TN 37212. International Copyright secured. All rights reserved. Used by permission.
8. Leo Buscaglia, *Living, Loving and Learning* (Thorndike, MA: Thorndike Press, 1982), 353–354.
9. From George Bernard Shaw, *The Devil's Disciple*, as quoted in *Familiar Quotations*, ed. John Bartlett (Boston: Little, Brown and Co., 1968), 836.
10. Doug Manning, *Don't Take My Grief Away* (San Francisco: Harper and Row Publishers, 1979), 50.
11. Betty Jane Wylie, *The Survival Guide for Widows* (New York: Ballantine Books, 1982), 115.
12. Mary Brite, *Triumph Over Tears* (Nashville: Thomas Nelson Publishers, 1979), 80.
13. Dag Hammarskjöld, *Markings* (New York: Knopf, 1964), 58.
14. Wylie, *The Survival Guide for Widows*, 114.
15. Brite, *Triumph Over Tears*, 38.
16. From Ambrose Bierce, *The Devil's Dictionary*, as quoted in *Familiar Quotations*, ed. John Bartlett (Boston: Little, Brown and Co., 1968), 791.
17. Haim Ginott, *Teacher and Child* (New York: The Macmillan Co., 1972), 280.
18. Manning, *Comforting Those Who Grieve*, 70.
19. David Augsburger, *Caring Enough to Hear* (Ventura, CA: Regal Books, 1982), 152.
20. Ewy, *Death of a Dream*, 80.
21. Ibid., 120.
22. Thomas Banville, *How To Listen—How To Be Heard* (Chicago: Nelson-Hall, 1978), 155.

Step 3: Attend the Service

1. Jill Krementz, *How It Feels When a Parent Dies* (New York: Alfred A. Knopf, 1981), 38.
2. Permission granted by the family members, who wish to remain anonymous.

3.   From John Donne "Holy Sonnets X," as quoted in *Familiar Quotations*, ed. John Bartlett (Boston: Little, Brown and Co., 1968), 308.

4.   Edgar N. Jackson, *When Someone Dies* (Philadelphia: Fortress Press, 1971), 26.

5.   Betty Jane Wylie, *The Survival Guide for Widows* (New York: Ballantine Books, 1982), 126–127.

6.   Ibid., 137.

7.   Jackson, *When Someone Dies*, 28–29.

8.   Harriet Sarnoff Schiff, *The Bereaved Parent* (New York: Penguin Books, 1971), 14.

9.   Krementz, *How It Feels When a Parent Dies*, 57.

10. Ibid., 54.

11. Nick Stinnett and John DeFrain, *Secrets of Strong Families* (New York: Berkley Books, 1986), 118.

Step 4: Give a Hug

1.   Interview with Dr. Norman Vincent Peale, January 28, 1987.

2.   From "Song of Myself," by Walt Whitman, *Leaves of Grass*.

3.   Oscar Wilde, *The Picture of Dorian Gray* (New York: Oxford University Press, 1981), Preface.

4.   Ashley Montagu, *Touching: The Human Significance of Skin* (New York: Columbia University Press, 1971), 31–35.

5.   Helen Colton, *The Gift of Touch* (New York: Seaview/Putnam, 1983), 119.

6.   Ibid., 117–118.

7.   Norman Cousins, *Anatomy of an Illness* (New York: W.W. Norton and Co., Inc., 1979), 154.

8.   David Bresler, as quoted in *Loving Each Other*, by Leo Buscaglia (Thorofare, NJ: Slack, Inc., 1984), 140.

9.   Betty Jane Wylie, *The Survival Guide for Widows* (New York: Ballantine Books, 1982), 113.

10. Lynn Caine, *Widow* (New York: William Morrow and Co., Inc., 1974), 11.

11. Fred Bauer, *Just a Touch of Nearness* (Norwalk, CT: The C.R. Gibson Co., 1985), 24-25.

Step 5: Write a Note

1. Mary Brite, *Triumph Over Tears* (Nashville: Thomas Nelson Publisher, 1979), 92.
2. Ibid., 93.
3. Ibid.
4. "Because He Lives," written by William J. and Gloria Gaither. Copyright 1971 by William J. Gaither. Used by Permission.
5. "His Eye Is on the Sparrow." Words by Savilla D. Martin and melody by Charles H. Gabriel. From Songs of Zion, Abingdon Press, Nashville, TN. Used by Permission.
6. Robert V. Ozment, *When Sorrow Comes* (Waco, TX: Word Books, Publisher, 1970), 50.
7. Norman Vincent Peale, *Wonderful Promises* (Carmel, NY: Guideposts, 1983), 32.
8. Phyllis Hobe, *Coping* (Caramel, NY: Guideposts, 1983), 233.
9. Corrie ten Boom, *Each New Day* (Old Tappan, NJ: Fleming H. Revell Co., 1977), 11.
10. William Blake, "On Another's Sorrow." In *Eerdmans' Book of Christian Poetry*, (Grand Rapids, MI: William B. Eerdmans Publishing Co., 1981). 45.
11. Brite, *Triumph Over Tears*, 95.

Step 6: Give a Gift

1. Material about Lynda Manning is based on interviews in 1987 and 1988 with Lorita Manning (Lynda's mother and my friend) and used by permission.
2. John DeFrain, Leona Martens, Jan Stork and Warren Stork, Stillborn: *The Invisible Death* (Lexington, MA: Lexington Books, 1986), book jacket.
3. Dorothy Corkille Briggs, *Embracing Life: Growing Through Love and Loss* (Garden City, NY: Doubleday and Co., Inc., 1985), 57.
4. Helen Keller, as quoted in Alan Loy McGinnis, *The Friendship Factor* (Minneapolis: Augsburg Publishing House, 1979), 23.
5. From Martin Farquhar Tupper, "Of Reading," Proverbial Philosophy, as quoted in *Familiar Quotations*, ed. John Bartlett (Boston: Little, Brown and Co., 1968), 658.

6. Catherine Lower O'Shea, "Someone to Share the Hurt," *Reader's Digest*, September 1987, 67–71.

7. Mary Brite, *Triumph Over Tears* (Nashville, TN: Thomas Nelson Publishers, 1979), 24–25.

8. Robert L. Montgomery, *Listening Made Easy* (New York: American Management Association, 1981), Preface.

9. Betsy Burnham, *When Your Friend Is Dying* (Grand Rapids, MI: Chosen Books of the Zondervan Corporation, 1982), 23.

Step 7: Extend an Invitation

1. Jill Krementz, *How It Feels When a Parent Dies* (New York: Alfred A. Knopf, 1981), 33.

2. Ibid., 110.

3. Ibid., 49–51.

4. Betty Jane Wylie, *The Survival Guide for Widows* (New York: Ballantine Books, 1982), 118.

5. Ibid., 106.

6. Judy Tatelbaum, *The Courage to Grieve* (New York: Harper and Row, Publishers, 1980), Prologue.

7. Harriet Sarnoff Schiff, *The Bereaved Parent* (New York: Penguin Books, 1983), 57.

8. Ibid.

9. Andor Foldes, "Beethoven's Kiss," *Reader's Digest*, November 1986, 145.

10. Charles R. Swindoll, *Dropping Your Guard* (Waco, TX: Word Books, Publisher, 1983), 127.

11. Tatelbaum, *The Courage to Grieve*, 43.

12. Ibid., 44.

13. William James, *Letters of William James*, Vol. 1, p. 249, to Carl Stumpf (January 1, 1886).

Appendix A

Actions to Take Before Death and Afterward

Before Death:

Regardless of your age or health status, collect information related to your death. Periodically update this information and keep it in a clearly labeled file or in a computer file (or both). Make the location of this information clear to your spouse, adult children, or whoever will be responsible for carrying out your wishes after your death. Include the following information/decisions:

1. Determine your wishes regarding the disposition of your body after death. Include your preferences for cremation, burial, and donating your body, tissues, and/or organs to help save lives and sight and to help train doctors, etc. If you choose to be buried, buy a burial plot for yourself and one for each of your family members. After making these decisions, give written copies to your spouse and children.

2. Keep your will updated and inform key family members of its location.

3. Inform key family members who the executor of your will is and who your attorney is.

4. Keep current lists of all your assets including bank accounts (checking and savings), retirement account(s), and other investments. Also keep current lists of all liabilities, such as charge accounts, credit card indebtedness, debt on your home, automobile loans, etc.

5. Decide on place of funeral or memorial service(s), who will officiate, what music you want, etc.

6. List the individuals you want to serve as pallbearers. Keep their contact information current.

7. Make a list of people to be notified upon your death including immediate family, close friends, and employer or business colleagues. Keep their contact information current.

8. Write your obituary, indicating date of birth, place of birth, occupation, college degrees, memberships held, military service, outstanding work, list of survivors in immediate family. As well as a written copy, store this information electronically if possible so changes and additions can be easily made after your death. Also store picture(s) that you want to use in your obituary.

9. DVDs, videos, and other presentations are increasingly used in services. If you prefer such a presentation, pick out pictures and/ or other items you wish included. Some funeral homes may have software for preparing presentations. Explore this possibility and get as much information, pictures, music selected, etc. as possible before your death.

10. Decide on appropriate memorial(s) to which gifts may be made, such as church, temple, synagogue, library, school, or specific charity.

11. Select clothes for the viewing; keep your selection current and location known to key person(s).

12. Make a list with contact information of all individuals that your executor or someone will need to contact after your death. Examples: your lawyer, your insurance companies, banks, Social Security office, etc.

13. Keep a current list of personal items that upon your death will be given to certain people. Examples: cherished memorabilia, rare book collection, valuable jewelry, etc.

After Death

If any of the foregoing actions were not taken before death, someone must carry them out after the death. Furthermore, the details of some actions may need attention that could not be given before the death. For example, the obituary will need completing by adding date and place of death, cause of death (optional), and date and location of the service, etc. After the death someone needs to:

1. Notify lawyer and executor.
2. Notify individuals selected to participate in the service, including officiating clergy, musicians, pallbearers, etc.
3. Arrange for members of family or close friends to take turns answering door and phone, keeping careful record of visitors and calls.
4. Arrange appropriate childcare.
5. Coordinate the supplying of food for the next days.
6. Consider special needs of the household, such as cleaning, etc.
7. Consider personal needs of the close survivor(s), such as sleeping accommodations, getting clothes ready, making hair appointments, etc. for family visitation and the service.
8. Arrange for security measures to be taken for the home of the deceased during the service and the time the deceased's family will be away from the home.
9. Plan for disposition of flowers after service (such as hospital or nursing home).
10. Prepare list of persons to receive acknowledgments for flowers, calls, etc.
11. Later assist in sending appropriate acknowledgments (can be written notes, printed acknowledgments, or some of each).
12. Request from the mortuary the number of needed copies of the death certificate.

13. Notify insurance companies.
14. Check with employer regarding unpaid compensation, death benefits, and annuity contracts.
15. Prepare list of distant persons to notify by email, letter, or printed notice, and decide which to send each. Prepare copy for printed notice if one is wanted.
16. Check carefully all life and casualty insurance and death benefits, including Social Security, credit union, trade union, fraternal, and military. Check also on income for survivor(s) from these sources.
17. Check promptly on all debts and installment payments. Some may carry insurance clauses that will cancel them. If there is to be a delay in meeting payments, consult with creditors and ask for more time before payments are due.
18. If deceased was living alone, notify utilities, landlord, post office etc. and notify them where to send mail etc.

Appendix B

Support Groups for the Bereaved*

AARP Grief and Loss Programs
601 E Street NW
Washington, DC 20049
www.aarp.org

> Works cooperatively with local organizations to develop community-based bereavement services. Programs include one-to-one outreach, group meetings (support groups, educational meetings, guest speakers, and online discussions), extensive Web site on coping with grief and loss, publications, referrals, and social activities.

American Cancer Society
1599 Clifton Road NE
Atlanta, GA 30329
(800) ACS-2345
www.cancer.org

> Local support groups for cancer patients and friends and family of individuals with cancer. The ACS also provides literature, workshops, and other resources for people experiencing the loss of a loved one.

American Foundation for Suicide Prevention
120 Wall Street, 22nd Floor
New York, NY 10005
www.afsp.org

> AFSP is the leading not-for-profit organization exclusively dedicated to understanding and preventing suicide through research and education, and to reaching out to people with mood disorders and those impacted by suicide. Provides a national directory of support groups for survivors. Suicide hot line: (800) 273-TALK (8255).

The Candlelighters
Childhood Cancer Foundation
3910 Warner Street
Kensington, MD 20895
www.candlelighters.org

> Network of peer support groups nationwide offers opportunities for members to socialize, solve problems, and share information. Also available are meetings, parent-to-parent visitation programs, summer camps, and publications.

Centering Corporation
1531 North Saddlecreek Road
Omaha, NE 68104
(866) 218-0101
www.centeringcorp.com

> The Centering Corporation is a non-profit organization dedicated to providing education and resources for the bereaved. *Grief Digest* is a new reader-friendly magazine that includes the best writers and speakers in the field of bereavement.

The Compassionate Friends
P. O. Box 3696
Oak Brook, IL 60522-3696
(630) 990-0010
www.compassionatefriends.org

> Nearly six hundred chapters nationwide. Self-help for bereaved parents, grandparents, and siblings. Meetings, conferences, books, pamphlets, and audio and video cassettes.

MADD (Mothers Against Drunk Driving)
P.O. Box 541688
Dallas, TX 75354-1688
(800) GET-MADD
www.madd.org

> A network of more than six hundred chapters (and forty professional

staff members) acting as a "voice" for victims of drunk drivers. Provides assistance with working through the courts and also a program of grief support. Provides crisis intervention and telephone counseling to those whose loved one has been killed in a drunk driving crash. 24-hour victim hotline: 800-438-6233.

National Hospice and Palliative Care Organization
1700 Diagonal Road, Suite 300
Alexandria, VA 22314
(800) 658-8898
www.nhpco.org

> Referral organization for local hospice programs for the terminally ill and the family.

Parents of Murdered Children, Inc. ®
100 East 8th Street
Suite B-41
Cincinnati, OH 45202
(888) 818-POMC
www.pomc.org

> National organization with local chapters. Educational programs and counseling for families of murdered children. Assistance includes support groups, newsletter, pamphlets, leaflets, reading lists, national conferences, and a memorial program. Special support at critical times in lives of survivors, such as at the trial of the child's accused murderer.

Parents Without Partners
1650 South Dixie Highway, Suite 510
Boca Raton, FL 33432
(561) 391-8833
www.parentswithoutpartners.org

> Chapters all across U. S. and Canada with affiliated organizations around the world. Mutual support group for single parents, including but not limited to the widowed parent. Local meetings, programs, brochures, and information sheets.

SHARE
Pregnancy and Infant Loss Support, Inc.
300 First Capitol Drive
St. Charles, MO 63301-2893
(800) 821-6819
www.nationalshareoffice.com

National network of local support groups. Publications, conferences, and telephone support for bereaved parents and other family members. Support for friends and others seeking information and understanding of the needs of the bereaved.

SIDS Alliance
1314 Bedford Ave
Suite 210
Baltimore, MD 21208
www.sidsalliance.org

National network of local chapters across the United States for parents and families who have lost a child to SIDS. Facilitates parent-to-parent contacts as well as seminars, workshops, printed materials, and other special services, including a national support center.

*There are support groups for almost all kinds of losses, such as Alzheimer's disease, muscular dystrophy, missing children, divorce, etc. Almost all have a Web site. For local chapters check the Web site, the telephone directory, and/or inquire of local clergy, hospitals, funeral directors, and/or social service directors.

Appendix C

Suggested Reading**

Albom, Mitch. *Tuesdays with Morrie*. Garden City, NY: Doubleday, 1997.

Bartocci, Barbara. *From Hurting to Happy: Transforming Your Life After Loss*. Notre Dame, IN: Ava Maria Press, 2002.

Brothers, Joyce. *Widowed*. NY: Ballantine Books, 1990.

Bauer, Fred. *Just a Touch of Nearness*. Norwalk, CT: The C. R. Gibson Co., 1985.

Biebel, David. *If God Is So Good, Why Do I Hurt So Bad?* Grand Rapids, MI: Fleming Revell Publishing, 1989.

Boss, Pauline. *Ambiguous Loss: Learning to Live with Unresolved Grief*. Cambridge, MA: Harvard University Press, 2000.

Briggs, Dorothy Corkille. *Embracing Life: Growing Through Love and Loss*. Garden City, NY: Doubleday, 1985.

Briggs, Lauren Littauer. "Grief and Loss," chapter thirteen in *Lives on the Mend*, Florence Littauer. Waco, TX: Word Books, Publisher, 1985.

Canfield, Jack and Mark Victor Hansen. *Chicken Soup for the Grieving Soul*. Deerfield Beach, FL: Health Communications, Inc., 2003.

Clairmont, Patsy. *Mending Your Heart in a Broken World: Finding Comfort in the Scriptures*. IN: Warner Press, 2002.

Clemons, Hardy. *Saying Goodbye to Your Grief*. Macon, GA: Smyth and Helwys Publishing, Inc., 1994.

Colson, Chuck, Max Lucado, and others. *Finding God's Peace in Perilous Times*. Wheaton, IL: Tyndale House Publishers, 2001.

Cowman, Charles E. *Streams in the Desert*. Uhrichville, OH: Barbour Publishing, 1998.

DeFrain, John, Leona Martens, Jan Stork, and Warren Stork. *Stillborn: The Invisible Death*. Lexington, MA: Lexington Books, 1986.

Dobson, James. *When God Doesn't Make Sense*. Wheaton, IL: Tyndale House Publishers, 2001.

Doka, Kenneth J., editor. *Living With Grief: Children, Adolescents and Loss*. Washington, D.C.: Hospice Foundation of America, 2000.

Doka, Kenneth J. and Joyce D. Davidson, editors. *Living With Grief at Work, at School, at Worship*. Washington, D.C.: Hospice Foundation of America, 2000.

Dunn, Ron. *When Heaven Is Silent*. Nashville, TN: Thomas Nelson Publishers, 1994.

Fitzgerald, Helen. *The Grieving Child*. NY: Simon and Schuster, 1994.

Fitzgerald, Helen. *The Mourning Handbook*. NY: Simon and Schuster, 1992.

Ford, Leighton. *Sandy: A Heart for God*. Minneapolis, MI: Grason, 1985.

Gilliam, Gwen and Barbara Russell Chesser. "How to Help an Accidental Killer," chapter ten in *Fatal Moments: The Tragedy of the Accidental Killer*. Lexington, MA: Lexington Books/D. C. Heath and Company, 1991.

Graham, Billy. "Happiness Through Showing Mercy," chapter six in *The Secret of Happiness*. Minneapolis, MI: Grason, 1985.

Gunther, John. *Death Be Not Proud*. NY: Harper Collins Publishers, 1998.

Hansen, Barbara. *Picking Up the Pieces: Healing Ourselves After Personal Loss*. NY: Harper Collins, Publishers, 1993.

Hayford, Jack. *How to Live Through a Bad Day*. Nashville, TN: Thomas Nelson Publishers, 2001.

Heavilin, Marilyn. "Death of a Child," chapter twelve in *Lives on the Mend*, Florence Littauer. Waco, TX: Word Books, Publisher, 1985.

Ilse, Sherokee. *Empty Arms: Coping After Miscarriage, Stillbirth, and Infant Death*. Maple Plain, MN: Wintergreen Press, 1992.

Ilse, Sherokee and Linda Hammer Burns. *Miscarriage: A Shattered Dream*. Maple Plain, MN: Wintergreen Press, 1992.

James, John W. and Frank Cherry. *The Grief Recovery Handbook*. NY: Harper and Row, Publishers, 1988.

Johnson, Joy. *Keys to Helping Children Deal With Death and Grief*. NY: Barron's Educational Series, Inc., 1999.

Kane, MD, Jeff. *The Healing Companion: Simple and Effective Ways Your Presence Can Help Heal People*. NY: Harper Collins Publishers, 2001.

Kaplan, Sandi and Gordon Lang. *Grief's Courageous Journey: A Workbook*. Oakland, CA: New Harbinger, 1995.

Katafiasz, Karen. *Finding Your Way Through Grief*. St. Meinrad, IN: Abbey Press, 1993.

Kinnaman, Gary. *My Companion through Grief*. Ann Arbor, MI: Servant Publications, 1996.

Kuenning, Delores. *Helping People through Grief.* Minneapolis, MN: Bethany House Publishers, 1987.

McNally, Shirley Reeser. *When Husbands Die.* Santa Fe, NM: Sunstone Press, 2005.

Manning, Doug. *Comforting Those Who Grieve.* San Francisco, CA: Harper and Row, Publishers, 1985.

Morris, Virginia. *Talking About Death.* Chapel Hill, NC: Algonquin Books, 2004.

Nystrom, Carolyn. *Emma Says Goodbye.* Batavia, IL: Lion Publishing Corporation, 1990.

Ogilvie, Lloyd J. *If God Cares, Why Do I Still Have Problems?* Minneapolis: Grason, 1985.

Parachin, Victor. *Grief Relief.* St. Louis, MO: Chalice Press. 1991.

Pausch, Randy with Jeffrey Zaslow. *The Last Lecture.* NY: Hyperion Books, 2008.

Peck, Rosalie and Charlotte Stefanics. *Learning to Say Goodbye.* Munci, IN: Accelerated Development, Inc., 1987.

Powell, Paul. *Death from the Other Side: Your Ministry to the Bereaved.* Dallas, TX: The Annuity Board, Southern Baptist Convention, 1991.

Raley, Helen Thames. *For Those Who Wait for Morning: Thoughts on Being a Widow.* Waco, TX: Word Books, Publisher, 1986.

Rando, Therese A. *How to Go on Living When Someone You Love Dies.* NY: Bantam Books, 1991.

Sittser, Gerald. *A Grace Disguised: How the Soul Grows Through Loss.* Grand Rapids, MI: Zondervan Publishing House, 1998.

Smolin, Ann and John Guinan. *Healing After the Suicide of a Loved One.* NY: Fireside/Simon and Schuster, 1993.

Stanley, Charles. *When Tragedy Strikes.* Nashville, TN: Thomas Nelson Publishing Co., 2001.

Stearns, Ann. *Living Through Personal Crisis.* NY: Ballantine Books, 1988.

Tatelbaum, Judy. *The Courage to Grieve.* NY: Harper and Row, Publishers, 1993.

Tenney, Tommy. *Trust and Tragedy: Encountering God in Times of Crisis.* Nashville, TN: Thomas Nelson Publishing Co., 2001.

Veninga, Robert. *A Gift of Hope.* Boston, MA: Little, Brown, and Co., 1985.

Walpole, Margaret. *Walking into the Morning: A Journey to the Other Side of Grief.* Norwalk, CT: C. R. Gibson, Co., 1986.

Walsh, Sheila. *Stones from the River of Mercy.* Nashville, TN: Thomas Nelson Publishing, 2000.

Watson, Jeffrey. *The Courage to Care: Helping the Aging, Grieving, and Dying*. Grand Rapids, MI: Baker Book House, 1992.

Wiersbe, Warren. W. and David Wiersbe. *Comforting the Bereaved*. Chicago, IL: Moody Press, 1985.

Yancey, Philip. *Where Is God When It Hurts?* Grand Rapids, MI: Zondervan Publishing House, 1992.

Zonnebelt-Smeenge, Susan J. and DeVries Robert C. *Getting to the Other Side of Grief*. Grand Rapids, MI: Baker Books, 1998.

Classics (published before 1985)

Allen, Charles L. *When You Lose a Loved One*. Westwood, NY: Fleming H. Revell Co., 1959.

Allen, Charles L. *The Miracle of Hope*. Old Tappan, NJ: Fleming H. Revell Co., 1973.

Anderson, Colena M. *Joy Beyond Grief*. Grand Rapids, MI: Zondervan Publishing House, 1979.

Bayly, Joseph. *The Last Thing We Talk About: Help and Hope for Those Who Grieve*. Elgin, IL: Chariot Family Publishers, 1973.

Berezin, Nancy. *After a Loss in Pregnancy: Help for Families Affected by a Miscarriage, a Stillbirth or the Loss of a Newborn*. NY: Simon and Schuster, 1982.

Blackburn, Bill. *What You Should Know about Suicide*. Waco, TX: Word Books, Publisher, 1982.

Borg, Susan and Judith Lasker. *When Pregnancy Fails*. Boston, MA: Beacon Press, 1981.

Brite, Mary. *Triumph Over Tears*. Nashville, TN: Thomas Nelson Publishers, 1979.

Burkle, Howard R. *God, Suffering and Belief*. Nashville, TN: Abingdon Press, 1977.

Claypool, John. *Tracks of a Fellow Struggler*. Waco, TX: Word Books, Publisher, 1976.

The Compassionate Friends. *Grieving, Healing, Growing*. Oak Brook, IL: The Compassionate Friends, 1982.

Decker, Beatrice and Gladys Kooiman. *After the Flowers Have Gone*. Grand Rapids, MI: Zondervan Publishing House, 1973.

DeFrain, John, Jacque Taylor and Linda Ernst. *Coping with Sudden Infant Death*. Lexington, MA: Lexington Books, 1982.

Dunlop, Richard S. *Helping the Bereaved*. Bowie, MD: The Charles Press Publishers, Inc., 1978.

Ewy, Donna and Rodger. *Death of a Dream*. NY: E.P. Dutton, Inc., 1984.

Fisher, Ida and Byron Lane. *The Widow's Guide to Life*. Englewood Cliff, NJ: Prentice Hall, 1981.

Glick, Ira O., Robert S. Weiss and C. Murray Parkes. *The First Year of Bereavement*. NY: John Wiley and Sons, 1974.

Grollman, Earl A. *Living When a Loved One Has Died*. Boston, MA: Beacon Press, 1977.

Grollman, Earl A. *Explaining Death to Children*. Boston, MA: Beacon Press, 1967.

Grollman, Earl A. *Concerning Death: A Practical Guide for the Living*. Boston, MA: Beacon Press, 1974.

Grollman, Earl A. *What Helped Me When My Loved One Died*. Boston, MA: Beacon Press, 1981.

Hewett, John H. *After Suicide*. Philadelphia, PA: Westminster Press, 1980.

Hobe, Phyllis. *Coping*. Carmel, NY: Guideposts, 1983.

Holmes, Majorie. *To Help You Through the Hurting*. Garden City, NY: Doubleday and Co., 1983.

Jackson, Edgar N. *Telling a Child about Death*. NY: Channel Press, 1965.

Jackson, Edgar N. *The Many Faces of Grief*. Nashville, TN: Abingdon Press, 1977.

Jackson, Edgar N. *When Someone Dies*. Philadelphia, PA: Fortress Press, 1971.

Jackson, Edgar N. *Understanding Grief*. Nashville, TN: Abingdon Press, 1957.

Jameson, Beth. *Hold Me Tight*. Old Tappan, NJ: Fleming H. Revell Co., 1971.

Jensen, Amy H. *Healing Grief*. Redmond, WA: Medic Publications Co., 1980.

Kohn, Jane Burgess and William K. Kohn. *The Widower*. Boston, MA: Beacon Press, 1978.

Koop, C. Everitt. *Sometimes Mountains Move*. Wheaton, IL: Tyndale House Publishers, 1979.

Krementz, Jill. *How It Feels When a Parent Dies*. NY: Alfred A. Knopf, 1981.

Kübler-Ross, Elisabeth. *On Children and Death*. NY: Macmillan Publishing Co., 1983.

Kübler-Ross, Elisabeth. *On Death and Dying*. NY: Macmillan Publishing Co., 1970.

Kübler-Ross, Elisabeth. *Questions and Answers on Death and Dying*. NY: Macmillan Publishing Co., 1974.

Kushner, Harold S. *When Bad Things Happen to Good People*. NY: Schocken Books, 1981.

Landorf, Joyce. *Mourning Song*. Old Tappan, NJ: Fleming H. Revell Co., 1974.

LeShan, Eda. *Learning to Say Good-bye: When a Parent Dies*. NY: Macmillan Publishing Co., 1978.

Lester, Andrew D. *It Hurts So Bad, Lord*. Nashville,TN: Broadman Press, 1976.

Lewis, C. S. *A Grief Observed*. London: Faber and Faber, 1961.

Liebman, Joshua L. "Grief's Slow Wisdom," chapter six in *Peace of Mind*. NY: Simon and Schuster, 1946.

Lindbergh, Anne Morrow. *Hour of Gold, Hour of Lead*. NY: Harcourt, Brace, Jovanovich, 1972.

Lindemann, Erich. *Beyond Grief*. NY: Jason Aronson, 1979.

Madden, Myron C. *Raise the Dead*. Waco, TX: Word Books, Publisher, 1975.

Manning, Doug. *Don't Take My Grief Away: What to Do When You Lose a Loved One*. San Francisco: Harper and Row, Publishers, 1979.

Marshall, Catherine. *To Live Again*. NY: McGraw-Hill Book Co., Inc., 1957.

Miller, William A. *When Going to Pieces Holds You Together*. Minneapolis, MI: Augsburg, 1976.

Morgan, Ernest. "Death Education," chapter one; "Living With Dying," chapter two, and "Bereavement," chapter three, in *Dealing Creatively with Death: A Manual of Death Education and Simple Burial*. Burnsville, NC: Celo Press, 1984.

Oates, Wayne E. "The Anxiety of Grief," chapter three in *Anxiety in Christian Experience*. Waco, TX: Word Books, Publisher, 1965.

Oates, Wayne E. *The Other Side of Anxiety*. Nashville, TN: Graded Press, 1975.

Oates, Wayne E. *Pastoral Care and Counseling in Grief and Separation*. Philadelphia, PA: Fortress Press, 1976.

Oates, Wayne E. *Your Particular Grief*. Philadelphia, PA: The Westminster Press, 1981.

Ozment, Robert V. *When Sorrow Comes*. Waco, TX: Word Books, Publisher, 1970.

Parkes, Colin M. *Bereavement Studies of Grief in Adult Life*. NY: International Universities Press, 1972.

Peale, Norman Vincent. *Wonderful Promises*. Carmel, NY: Guideposts, 1983.

Pincus, Lily. Death and the Family: *The Importance of Mourning*. NY: Vintage Books, 1974.

Price, Eugenia. *Getting Through the Night: Finding Your Way after the Loss of a Loved One*. NY: The Dial Press, 1982.

Price, Eugenia. *No Pat Answers*. Carmel, NY: Guideposts, 1972.

Rogers, Dale Evans with Floyd Thatcher. *God in the Hard Times of Death*. Waco, TX: Word Books, Publisher, 1984.

Rowley, Carol A. and William J. *On Wings of Mourning*. Waco, TX: Word Books, Publisher, 1984.

Schiff, Harriet S. *The Bereaved Parent*. NY: Crown Publications, 1977.

Schuller, Arvella. "When the Family Faces Crises," chapter nine in *The Positive Family*. NY: Doubleday and Co., Inc., 1982.

Skoglund, Elizabeth. *Coping: Insights from Amy Carmichael, C. S. Lewis, Charles Spurgeon, and Hudson Taylor*. Ventura, CA: Regal Books, 1971.

Stearns, Ann Kaiser. *Living Through Personal Crisis*. NY: Ballantine Books, 1984.

Stone, Howard W. *Suicide and Grief*. Philadelphia, PA: Fortress Press, 1972.

Stringfellow, William. *A Simplicity of Faith: My Experiences in Mourning*. Nashville, TN: Abingdon Press, 1982.

Swindoll, Charles. *For Those Who Hurt*. Portland, OR: Multnomah Publishers, 1977.

Switzer, David K. *The Dynamics of Grief*. Nashville, TN: Abingdon Press, 1970.

Tournier, Paul. "Suffering," chapter eleven in *The Healing of Persons*. NY: Harper and Row, Publishers, 1965.

Towns, James E. *Faith Stronger Than Death*. Anderson, IN: Warner Press, 1975.

Westberg, Granger E. *Good Grief*. Philadelphia, PA: Fortress Press, 1962.

Wiersbe, Warren W. *Why Us? When Bad Things Happen to God's People*. Old Tappan, NJ: Fleming H. Revell Co., 1984.

Wolf, Anna. *Helping Your Child to Understand Death*. NY: Child Study Press, 1973.

Wylie, Betty Jane. *The Survival Guide for Widows*. NY: Ballantine Books, 1982.

Young, Amy L. *By Death or Divorce: It Hurts to Lose*. Denver, CO: Accent Books, 1976.

Zundel, Veronica. *Eerdman's Book of Famous Prayers*. Grand Rapids, MI: William B. Eerdman's Publishing Co., 1983.

**Some of these books may be out of print. However, they can be found in libraries, ordered through inter-library loan, or purchased from companies with web sites that sell out-of-print books such as Amazon.com, Alibris.com, AbeBooks.com, etc.

LaVergne, TN USA
16 June 2010
186286LV00003B/3/P